LETTERS FROM THE TEACHER

TEACHINGS OF
THE ORDER OF CHRISTIAN MYSTICS

LETTERS FROM THE TEACHER

Teachings of The Order of Christian Mystics

The "Curtiss Books" freely available at

www.orderofchristianmystics.co.za

1. The Voice of Isis
2. The Message of Aquaria
3. The Inner Radiance
4. Realms of the Living Dead
5. Coming World Changes
6. The Key to the Universe
7. The Key of Destiny
8. Letters from the Teacher Volume I
9. Letters from the Teacher Volume II
10. The Truth about Evolution and the Bible
11. The Philosophy of War
12. Personal Survival
13. The Pattern Life
14. Four-Fold Health
15. Vitamins
16. Why Are We Here?
17. Reincarnation
18. For Young Souls
19. Gems of Mysticism
20. The Temple of Silence
21. The Divine Mother
22. The Soundless Sound
23. The Mystic Life
24. The Love of Rabiacca
25. Potent Prayers

Supporting Volumes

26. The Seventh Seal
27. Towards the Light

Letters from the Teacher
(Of the Order of The 15)

Transmitted by

RAHMEA

Priestess of the Flame

Edited by

F. HOMER CURTISS, B.S., M.D.

Secretary of the Order

VOL. I.

2013 EDITION

REPUBLISHED FOR THE ORDER
BY MOUNT LINDEN PUBLISHING
JOHANNESBURG, SOUTH AFRICA
ISBN: 978-1-920483-17-3

Dedication

To that Great Teacher

who brought the Wisdom-Religion

to the Western World,

known on earth as

HELENA   PETROVNA   BLAVATSKY

this volume is affectionately dedicated by her

loving pupils and disciples,

        Pyrahmos and Rahmea.

"Ministers of Christ and Stewards of the Mysteries of God."
1 Corinthians 4 vs. 1

COPYRIGHT 2013

BY
MOUNT LINDEN PUBLISHING

First Published in 1909

May be used for non-commercial, personal, research and educational use.
ALL RIGHTS RESERVED

Preface

The Letters from the Teacher of THE ORDER OF THE 15, in answer to questions from pupils, are of such universal interest to seekers after Wisdom that we consider them far too valuable to be confined merely to the ones to whom they were addressed. Therefore we make available extracts from the more important ones.

With a few exceptions the selection has been confined to those received during the first six months of the work (January to June, 1908). But even these few cover a wide field and deal with a diversity of subjects not dealt with elsewhere in the same frank and common-sense way. Hence they fill a distinct want in occult literature.

The letters are genuine extracts from originals still in possession of the Secretary; but in many cases the Editor has taken the liberty of condensing the spirit of a letter into a simple question.

The literary faults are those of the Editor.

THE EDITOR.

Table of Contents

Part I.	The Masters of Wisdom and Their Work...	4
Part II.	Concerning THE ORDER OF THE 15. . .	23
Part III.	Prayer.	33
Part IV.	The Astral Plane.	39
Part V.	Phenomena.	58
Part VI.	Dreams and Visions.	64
Part VII.	Health and Disease.	68
Part VIII.	The Sex Problem.	82
Part IX.	Spiritual Growth and Development.	104
Part X.	Miscellaneous.	138

PART I

THE MASTERS OF WISDOM AND THEIR WORK

"If there are in the Universe such beings as Angels or Spirits, whose INCORPOREAL essence may constitute an intelligent Entity, notwithstanding the absence of any (to us) solid organism; and if there are those who believe that a God made the first man out of dust, and breathed into him a living Soul—and there are millions upon millions who believe both—what does this doctrine of ours contain that is so impossible?"

—Blavatsky, THE SECRET DOCTRINE, Vol. II.

June 1st, 1908.
"Since I was about fourteen years of age, I've been a church member and worker therein, always loving it because it is God's work. . . . I have been the recipient of a communication from you relative to the ORDER OF THE 15. It is entirely new matter to me, so I should be glad for you to write to me and explain the meaning of 'Masters of Wisdom' and 'Great White Lodge'."

The Masters of Wisdom are Great Souls who, through repeated experiences and determined effort through many earth lives, have obtained mastery firstly over the passions, appetites and desires of the personal self, and secondly over the forces of Their bodies and over the life-currents of the cosmos. Hence They have become one with the Fount of all Wisdom. They and the Father are one. Jesus was such a Master, in fact was and IS a Master of Masters. But there are many more, all banded together in what is known as THE GREAT WHITE LODGE; a lodge in the sense of oneness of aim and motive; for They are all working for the upliftment of humanity. They are divided into certain degrees and subdivided into orders so as to systematically cover all the needs of humanity in its different stages of evolution. You will thus see that there are Masters of all grades, that is, upon all steps of the ladder leading to the point of highest attainment where a Master of Masters stands. Each group and each individual has a certain work to do for the betterment of humanity. These Great Souls are able to function on all planes, hence They are near to all who really need Their help; for humanity must reach out for help ere it can be given. As long as individuals are satisfied with a purely physical existence the Masters know well that they are not yet ready to be helped; for their lessons are those of the physical. So They wait patiently through the ages, knowing that all is well, and that the treading of the downward arc of the cycle, while apparently leading away from Godhood, in reality is leading the Soul to a necessary point where, having fed on the husks and consorted with the swine, it lifts up its eyes and sees afar off its Father's home and says, "I will arise and go to my father." It is here that some helping hand is always stretched out to them, and it is always from the Lodge of Masters, who have been watching and waiting in patient love for that moment, that the help comes. It may seem to come from some natural and ordinary source, but in reality it is from these Watchers and Elder Brothers of humanity who make use of natural channels to answer the cry of the Soul for light and help.

As the Soul evolves upward and inward it will take many decided steps; will reach points where all the old props which seemed so satisfying will drop away like the straws that elude the grasp of a drowning man. This simply means that the Soul has entered a new Order, and that which helped in the old grade or Order is now no longer sufficient. The Soul cries out in dismay, "Help, Lord, or I perish!" Then it is that the outward recognition comes, just as these new teachings are coming to you. The Masters of Wisdom know who need the outer help, and it never fails to present itself. It is no new teaching nor a getting away from Christianity and the Savior; it is but a new step on The Path; a higher grade in the school of the Soul; a drawing nearer to the only Savior, The Christ who dwells forever among men—aye in their very midst. One of the aims of this Order is the expounding of the teachings of the Master Jesus, and we trust that the above outline will help you to grasp something of its significance.

May 13th, 1908.

"In the existence of Masters I joyfully believe, but that there are also astral entities masquerading as Masters I believe as well. How are we going to know the difference? So far, apparently, the wisdom of the. . . . is quite unable to help us on this point, for at present that society presents the unedifying spectacle of intelligent men and women prostrate under the glamor of the most morbid and unhealthy character, blindly following beings who, if we are to judge them by the words given to us as theirs, are thoroughly erratic and unreliable, and indeed, disreputable. These are the Masters of a large portion of the. . . . !"

We are not surprised at your attitude, for it is quite natural under the circumstances. But when you come to grasp the significance of all the seeming confusion of which you complain you will understand that it is the necessary working out of the Great Law as expressed in THE VOICE OF THE SILENCE, viz., " 'Great Sifter' is the name of the 'Heart Doctrine,' O Disciple. The wheel of the Good Law moves swiftly on. It grinds by night and by day. The worthless husks it drives out from out the golden grain, the refuse from the flour. The hand of Karma guides the wheel; the revolutions mark the beating of the cosmic heart."

The ----- , and its subsidiary the -----, as well as many other bona fide movements, were started for the express purpose of testing and selecting the wheat from the chaff. This explains the many upheavals and troubles that have come to all these movements; they are but the threshing of the grain. This has been going on for its appointed time and now the winnowing process has begun. This Movement is but one more stroke of the flail. Being nearer the end the strokes come quicker and heavier, and all the grains must feel the blows; but with them comes the skill and strength of the Great Sifter who already discerns the golden grain and directs His strokes with wisdom, so that no true grain will be crushed or lost. "Shun ignorance, and likewise shun illusion. Avert thy face from world deceptions." Many are called, truly, but few are chosen.

As you say, the leaders may have proof of the presence of the Master, yet each student must find and prove that Presence for himself. The whole aim and end of this Movement is to help each individual Soul to find, not only The Christ within himself, but also the guiding hand of the Master. We cannot assure you that you will find Him, for many feel around in a darkness created by themselves and never touch the outstretched hand. To quote again, "For mind is like a mirror; it gathers dust while it reflects. It needs the gentle breezes of Soul-wisdom to brush away the dust of our illusions." We can only say that the Teacher and Guide stands ready, close at hand, to guide and help you through this labyrinth of darkness into the light of the perfect day.

May 6th, 1908.

"I am desirous of associating with you as closely as I may be permitted, so that you may teach me how to better understand the law of our eternal Being and help humanity."

The Lodge of Masters is eagerly watching and waiting for the development of every avenue through which They can pour love and wisdom to enlighten the world in this its darkest hour; the hour that precedes the dawn of the coming day. In exact proportion to the true Soul-desire for light, and the practical effort toward the purification and sanctification of the instrument, will you become "a center through which the Lodge can work." "Blessed are they who hunger and thirst after righteousness, for they SHALL be FILLED." Meditate upon the PRAYER OF CONSECRATION.[1] Study it line by

---

[1] See Appendix.

line and word by word until you get a realization of its meaning.

May 2nd, 1908.
"Please tell me what you mean by the Shining Ones you mentioned in your previous letter."

The Shining Ones are called by various names, according to their seven degrees or divisions, from the Elohim and the Devas down to the Nature Sprites and Elementals. The lower orders (elementals) are creating the forms of nature, while the higher orders (Angels) are the builders of man's higher, spiritual body through which he must ultimately express his Higher Self. "They are 'Gods THE CREATURES' while he (the Supreme. Ed.) is 'God THE CREATOR'. . . . More brilliant than flames, more rapid than the wind, and they live in love and harmony, mutually enlightening each other, feeding on the bread and a mystic beverage—the communion wine and water?—surround as with A RIVER OF FIRE the throne of the Lamb, and veiling their faces with their wings. This throne of love and glory they leave only to carry to the stars, the earth, the kingdoms and all the sons of God, their brothers and pupils, in short, all creatures like themselves, the divine influence."[1]

The spiritual or **NIRMANAKAYA** body is the Fire-body that is builded slowly and gradually, cell by cell, by each Soul throughout its incarnations. It is not something attained at the time of death or at the time of triumph, but all along The Path. In each body informed by the Ego there are some few atoms, more or less, which have been redeemed by him, and it is these atoms (whether physical, mental or spiritual) that the Angels—the Shining Ones—gather and hold and manipulate, under karmic law, into the final glorified body in which there is no death, because each molecule and cell has been purified in the fire and redeemed forever more. This is "the Nirmanakaya's humble robe" in which the Soul clothes itself when it has taken the final step. It is these redeemed atoms that the Angels gather, even at the expense of the unredeemed.

May 18th, 1908.
"I have been in search of my Higher Self or the Cosmic Consciousness that I have read so much about but seen so little of its manifestation by those who make such great claims of having realized the Inner Light. . . . My last experience has been with. . . . who claims to be an Initiate of the

---

[1] SECRET DOCTRINE, Blavatsky, Vol. III, p. 207.

Great White Lodge, and I was under the training of a so-called Master for 18 months, with the result that my wife became a nervous and mental wreck. . . . At present I am studying with Mr. . . . of New York but his prices are so high that it nearly prevents me from going any farther. . . . In my case I have paid out hundreds of dollars and given 20 years of time, and have lived to the best of my understanding a pure and spiritual life, yet the further and deeper I go the darker seems to be the path."

You are indeed wandering round and round the endless circle of existence seeking on the outer rim that which can only be found within, at the very germinal point of the mundane egg. You cry: "Lo! Here! Lo! there!" and are seeking, seeking everywhere, while all the time the Divine One stands close to you and with outstretched arms cries: "Come unto me and rest thou weary and heavy laden!"

You can set it down for a positive fact that no Master of Wisdom ever did, ever will or ever could advertise Himself or give out spiritual teachings at so much per lesson. Nor is there any such thing as an Initiate of the Great White Lodge upon the physical plane acting in His physical body, and claiming to be such. The Great White Lodge does not work that way. If there were such an Initiate thus working you would probably never find it out; for He would go about, like the Master Jesus, among the sick and poor, and be despised of men— His works alone proclaiming Him. Neither can money buy the gifts of God. You remember the rebuke given to Simon when he offered money to the disciples for those gifts? "Thy money perish with thee, because thou hast thought that the gift of God can be purchased with money. Thou hast neither part nor lot in this matter, for thy heart is not right in the sight of God."[1] No one can claim to give spiritual development. Only the Soul itself can earn it. And how dare one take money for that which is not his to give? The very claim of being able to give such gifts for money proclaims the impostor.

Do not confuse THE ORDER OF THE 15 with any such claims. This Order is put forth by the Lodge of Masters; but we make no personal claims as to being Masters, or even Initiates, or anything but human beings who have reached a point where The Lodge can work through us. This Order, being the result of the normal evolution of humanity, is, of necessity, un-

---

[1] While it is now recognized that this saying is an interpolation made by the early church fathers, nevertheless it illustrates the point. – Ed.

der the direct and special guidance of the Masters of Wisdom from the higher planes. Its mission is to awaken in the minds of those who are waiting and seeking for light, a desire to seek within. It is proposed to give such assistance to humanity, through human agents who are willing to devote their time and energy without compensation, as will help all Souls who are ready to step onward, upward and inward.

All persons laying claim to being Masters of Wisdom or Initiates must, of necessity, come under the law governing such advanced Beings. And at the very Threshold of Initiation they must be confronted with the sacrifice of all personal ambitions and worldly preferments; for these must be given up ere victory can be won. "Ye cannot serve God and mammon" was spoken directly to neophytes seeking Initiation, and was not given to the general run of mankind. The law is imperative and inviolable; once having renouced all worldly honor as the price of the power to be won, they CANNOT, if they would, demand a money price for their services; for that would at once put them outside The Lodge force, and no gifts would be theirs to impart. "Freely ye have received, freely give" was another direction given by the Master Jesus to His immediate disciples who were candidates for Initiation, and it applies to all. The gifts of God are free, and are given only to the sincere seeker, the Law of Compensation demanding as a price that he shall freely give, i.e., to give (not pay) to others of his time, love, sympathy, money—of all he has—to spread the good tidings; never to enrich one person who claims all power. If, after the solemn services and obligations of Initiation, a neophyte should take pay for what is not his to give (for at most he is but an agent—a transmitter of the Gifts of God entrusted to him to distribute) he becomes a deserter and a reprobate. All that ANY agent dare claim is just compensation for money expended, or to be the custodian of money given for the spread of the work.[1]

The sad condition of your wife is, unfortunately, a very common result of this serving of Mammon—the Beast spoken of in Revelation – under the name of The Christ; for that is what it is to demand pay for spiritual gifts. While most students accept the fact that the Beast is the money power, yet there is a failure to realize things literally, especially the fact that the Revelation of St. John was a true prophecy[1] which in this day is being fulfilled. If this is true, then, surely, it is well to take to heart the message of the third Angel who cried with a loud voice: "If any man worship the Beast and his image and receive his mark in his forehead or in his hand, the same shall drink of the wine of the wrath of God." To worship the Beast, however, does not mean that we are not to give money its proper place; we worship it by exalting it above all else. In the present state of the world, i.e., during the reign of the Beast, we must, of necessity, use the coin of the realm, yet we—especially such as claim to be the spiritual guides and teachers of others—must be very careful not to have the mark of the Beast on our hands or foreheads.

The lesson of your wife's affliction is that all forced development—and all is forced that is being supposedly given at so much per lesson—is like forcibly tearing open a rose-bud. The more sensitive and highly attuned the one receiving such treatment, the more dire the results. No growth is normal or lasting except that which follows the law of natural growth "He that doeth the will of the Father." We will do all that is possible to help your wife; but again we must warn you that, as it has been the result of abnormal conditions, her return to health must be slow and must follow the line of natural spiritual growth and development.

Feb. 12th, 1908.

"I have just finished reading a book entitled 'The Crucifixion' which refutes the death of Christ while on the cross. . . . What do you think of it?"

The book about which you ask may, or may not, be true; but it makes very little difference, as far as the truth of His teachings is concerned, whether or not such a man as Jesus ever lived. As a matter of history, there was a high Initiate of that name who did pass through the experiences symbolized in the Bible during the pilgrimage of His Soul toward mastery, just as every Soul must pass that way. But the whole story, as it is told, is one grand allegory[2] designed to teach, exoterically, the inner truths of the different steps on The Path. Each step has its trials and sufferings, its mockery of the multitude and the final crucifixion of the lower personality on the cross,[3] and the glorious resurrection into life immortal; the triumph of the spiritual over the temporal man. The story is woven around

---

[1] Altho copied almost bodily from the BOOK OF ENOCH, which in turn was but a transcript from far older texts.—Ed.
[2] See lesson CONCERNING THE DOCTRINE OF HELL-FIRE.
[3] See lesson THE MEANING OF THE CROSS.

this Initiate, Jesus, and events and places are adapted or created to carry out the symbology; but every name used, as well as every incident, has its inner meaning when interpreted kabalisticly. This is the style after which all scriptures are written, i.e., the Vedas, Upanishads, etc. It is the method always adopted by Initiates in giving out the great truths so that only those who have developed the qualities necessary to the true understanding can see the inner meaning. The multitude see the beautiful story, which always contains a sound moral lesson, and each one gets from it exactly what he is ready to receive. The man Jesus may never have died upon a cross, in fact He may have lived to an advanced age and have lain down the earth life when He was ready to enter the higher; but it makes little difference either way, for it is His teachings that count. And they remain today the most beautiful ever given to man. Some day, perhaps, we will be given His actual history as a man; but it is of little moment. Take the lesson intended by the allegory and "live the life."

May 30th, 1908.

"I am much interested to know just why the Master of the Order could not tell me more about the psychical experience to which I referred in my last letter. . . . I confess that I sent the question to you partly as a test and partly because I would really be grateful for more information regarding the experience."

If it were desirable to give a mediumistic "test" it could easily be done, even without the overshadowing of the Master. This, however, is far from the idea of this Movement. The ORDER OF THE 15 is put forth to feed the heart-hunger, to assist the weary Soul to enlightenment, and to help to a better understanding all who are looking for love and sympathy and help. The Master knows very well what the lesson was that was given to you by the experience of which you speak; but no one except yourself can know the exact interpretation you have given to it unless it is filched from your mind by a mediumistic trick. Until you give your version, in a heartfelt desire to obtain help in understanding the lesson, the Master cannot help you. In fact, if you are satisfied that you have gotten it straight and that there is no more to it and only ask as a "test," then there is no need to help you; you do not want it, and the lesson given has failed.

April 11th, 1908.
"I have a brother who disappeared about 1898 and has never been positively heard from since then. . . . Is it within your power or right to help me find him if alive, and reunite him to his sisters?"

As to your brother's whereabouts, this cannot be revealed to you at the present time. It is not expedient for the Masters to interfere with the personal Karma of any individual. He must be permitted to work out his problems in his own way. But while he is working them out he is guided and helped, and advantage is taken of every opening that will aid him in learning his lessons. This does not mean that you are not to do your best to find and help him; but when you have done your best leave the rest in the hands of your Father in Heaven.

Feb. 21st, 1908.
"I'm in some doubt as to whether I belong to the sheep or the goats, but as your circular is 'to those who truly desire to progress' I may classify myself in that category. . . . From my many occult experiences the conviction was forced upon me that humanity as a whole is practically under hypnotic control. . . . At one time I thought that those Deities who are the most intimately related to the evolution of every ego, yet who have the power to flout discovery of Themselves, did not know Their business as well as I!!! I was given great truths but was told that the time was not ripe for their publication. I insisted nevertheless that I would tell what I had perceived. My article was put in type, but in some way they neglected to let me read the proof. When I saw the article in print words were misspelled or pied and lines transposed so that it was impossible for anyone to guess what I meant to say. Those Deities, Beings, Adepts had verified my conception of Their power, and at the same time effectually blocked my effort to disclose Their identity."

It makes very little difference whether or not you belong to the sheep or the goats. Each has his own place and his own work. One makes good mutton, while the other affords a grand lesson in fortitude, contentment with whatever food comes along and a maintenance of a persevering determination to climb to the very top and surmount every difficulty.

There is much still for you to learn, and there is no one more in need of careful training and guidance than one who has found entrance to the inner planes while still unable to fully grasp and correlate the teachings received. Especially is this true of one who, in his great desire to give out to the world that which fills him with ecstasy, is yet impatient of restraint, and who lacks the ability to classify to such an extent that the results would do more harm to humanity than good. For instance, your surmise that humanity is under hypnotic control, if given out to the world, would be a death blow to progress and would stultify all effort to conquer on the part of all who accepted it. When you are able to see farther you will understand why. In the present condition of humanity, to a superficial glance, it might look as though they were but a mass of puppets moved by wires manipulated by those on other planes; but this is only the result of man's long continued refusal to live up to his real possibilities and his consequent loss of certain powers. Behind it is the grand truth of FREE WILL. But, alas, man himself has erected barriers, has subordinated his powers and debased his understanding and given over control of both his mind and his actions to entities who must, through karmic right, hold the reins until man once more awakens to his Divine heritage, and once more takes the guidance upon himself. . . .

Do you not have faith enough to believe that those Masters who have devoted Their all to the advancement of humanity know, better than your finite mind could possibly comprehend, what will benefit humanity most? And what, by being trampled in the mire, will but add to the karmic burden of humanity? Your attitude of desiring to rush into print with what is given you personally is as foolish as if you insisted on feeding a fever patient with a newly discovered food when the doctors told you not to.

May 8th, 1908.
"When I said the human kingdom overlapped the animal kingdom through the anthropoid ape there was no connection in my mind with any of the degrees of The Lodge. Will you please explain?"

The anthropoid ape, being the degenerate offspring of man—the result of his cohabitation with antedeluvian (Atlantean) monsters—has in it the spark of Manas, and hence belongs, to that extent, to the human kingdom. Therefore, it must be under the direct guidance of the 7th degree of The Lodge during its evolution; for no entity can obtain mastery and final liberation until all the atoms for whose expression he is responsible, have been redeemed. This includes all the atoms thrown off from all his various bodies during all his incarnations, as well as all the entities he has created either with his physical creative force or by the creative power of thought. It is only then that he has finished his "cycle of necessity." When a

Great Soul reaches the Threshold of Mastery he realizes that he is mysteriously connected with and responsible for a host of entities in almost every stage of development on all the lower planes. Hence the septenary division of the work of The Lodge into degrees and sub-degrees, each under the guidance of certain Masters, so that all may be cared for and helped in exact justice. It is very like a school divided into grades, and each grade into classes, each under a different teacher, yet all subject to the Principal, and he in turn to the Commissioner of Education.

April 29th, 1908.
"I have been given some duties to perform in the way of exercises given out by Master. . . . , which I cannot perform as I would owing to too much work for others. The chase for bread and butter is so great that it takes nearly all my time. I have to work from 10 to 14 hours a day in a saw-mill and you can see that it keeps me 'goin' some."

We note what you say about performing exercises, but think you must have made some mistake as to their source; for no Master would ever give to a pupil exercises of a physical nature that would be likely to overtax his capacity. You can readily understand that such exercises cannot be given out in a general way, but each lesson must be adapted to the personal development of the student, thus they would not be such as to overtax his capacity for performance. The Masters of Wisdom know well the physical conditions as well as the spiritual development of each pupil, and the Law of Growth is always followed; each pupil must learn to correlate with his special environment.

Anything that would tend to retard or prevent you from doing your plain duty in that condition and position in life in which the great Law of Karma has placed you, would be a serious setback to your spiritual development and hence such directions would never be given by a Master of Wisdom. We can never conquer a thing until we have worked it out, and to take up YOGI exercises when your strength is fully taxed to perform your necessary physical labor is to crowd out something which should come first—something which lies nearer. People often make the mistake of saying that some Master requires a certain thing of them when, as a matter of fact, they have never received any direct, personal instructions from a Master. You can apply this test to instructions received from any source: Are they reasonable? are they just? are they right? Directions for physical exercises are never given by a Master of Wisdom except in a personal way, and in such a case they would be adapted to that pupil's ability and capacity, and to that pupil alone.

May 19th, 1908.
"I am pleased with the titles Teachers, Guides, Elder Brothers, but the title 'Masters' grates on my nerves. I long to see this world without a master or a slave in it."

We understand and appreciate your attitude. You are suffering from a very common, and a very natural, misunderstanding of the term mentioned owing to the common use and abuse of the word Master by many so-called followers of the Wisdom-Religion. Jesus, who was the greatest Initiate (Master) the world has ever known, said: "One is your master even Christ: and all ye are brethren. Neither be ye called masters: for one is your master even Christ. When the expression "Masters of Wisdom" is used, reference is had to this very thing. Masters are Beings who, through much travail of Soul, have attained the Christ center where The Christ has regained His rightful place as Master of all the forces, molecules and powers that compose mortal bodies—physical, astral and men—The Christ in command is the Master.

It is erroneous to use the expression "my Master" or "your Master," for, as Jesus pointed out, no MAN can be your master. When you have gained mastery over the kingdom given to you yourself, with its sheaths or bodies, by your Father, then do you become a Master. Again, Jesus said, "Ye have been faithful over a few things, (i.e. your emotions, words, acts, etc.) behold I (The Christ) will make you ruler (Master) over many. Think this matter over. Meditate especially upon the text given that "All ye are brethren". You have recognized the point to which humanity has struggled and should have faith to know that whenever such a point is reached an effort is made to bring back the disobedient wanderers to the true center; to prepare at least a few who will and can recognize the necessity for the coming of a direct Savior or Avatar—a perfected Soul such as the Master Jesus. This has never yet failed in the history of the world, and, as you say, conditions are ripe at the present time for such another coming. Think you that there will now be the first failure? The cry of every sincere heart for light and upliftment shall be answered, and at the present time the cry from many, many hearts is calling continually, day and night: "How long Lord? How long?" And the answer comes: "While they are yet speaking, I will hear."

June 1st, 1908.

"If the Persian teacher called The Bab is a Master why does he not teach reincarnation and Karma?"

The Bab is a very high Master. In fact he is an Emanation or Personification of the coming Avatar or World Savior. That is, the mortal body of a Persian youth has been overshadowed and informed by The Christos to such a degree that it manifests The Christ. Such a manifestation, however, must of necessity, work through a physical body sufficiently purified, and a brain sufficiently trained to become an instrument through which The Christ can work to an exceptional degree. The Bab is a Persian, with all the national leadings and tendencies that appeal to that race, who has been especially prepared to be an instrument through which The Christ can come to the Mohammedans. It is a case of Avesha Avatara, the overshadowing and informing of the lesser by the greater. As one writer says "In the Avesha Avatara a pure vessel is chosen, not necessarily a MUKTA YOGI (a liberated man), and the Divine Life utilizes the Man thus qualified, for a limited period and for a particular purpose. . . . Generally, for a life time, the Divine Influence continues to shine through the purified vessel and, to all appearances, as in reality it is, the human nature of the man is submerged by the overflowing Divine Life."[1] In such cases nothing of the individuality is lost; it is the personality plus the higher principles of some Great Teacher, or say of The Christ. Such overshadowing is by no means as rare as may be supposed, the difference being in the advancement of the overshadowing, or we might say, incarnating Teacher, who, in all such cases, projects His higher principles (Atma, Buddhi, Manas) into, or grafts them upon, the individuality of the disciple who, through his own choice and purity of life, has prepared a mentality and a personality capable of expressing the Great Soul who descends thus to help humanity.

As to the Bab's teaching Reincarnation and Karma, it is given to every Great Teacher to use His own judgment as to the amount and the method of giving out the Divine Teachings. Also, being a Persian, the brain-mind of the personality or in-

---

[1] Studies in THE BHAGAVAD GITA, III series, p. 130.

strument used does not respond to the truths mentioned and does not make them a reality, as would be the case with a disciple who had been trained in that line of thought. The Teacher overshadowing the Bab does not think the Persians, or rather the Mohammedans in general, are ready for the teaching of Reincarnation. And when you think of the materialism of the Mohammedans you will not wonder at this decision; for such a teaching would be too great a jump from their previous race-training and habits of thought and would tend to confuse instead of to unify them. Therefore that Teacher teaches such ethics of life as will prepare them to overcome their Karma and be ready for Reincarnation. He teaches immortality, but does not specify. Perhaps some of his followers may be led to deny Reincarnation, because it is not found in his teachings; but the Bab himself does not deny it, he simply does not realize it because the overshadowing entity ignores it, thinking that his children are not yet ready for it and that, if they follow his teachings and make their lives conform to them, Reincarnation will take care of itself. No one is ready to learn Reincarnation to whom it does not appeal. Only those who feel an inward urge to know THE WHOLE truth need have it given them. The Bab is giving the Mohammedans all they can grasp and live up to.

The Bab is not a direct Avatar or World Savior, but is the Savior for the Mohammedans. Those of the Western world who feel especially drawn to his teachings are probably reincarnated Mohammedans and naturally come under his magnetic influence.

Each sub-race has a direct Avatar who embodies the highest ideals of that sub-race. The Avatar is always in advance of the sub-race to which He comes, being the highest type to which the sub-race, as a sub-race, can evolve. The coming Avatar for the new sub-race (the sixth), now evolving in the Western hemisphere, will represent the highest possibilities of the sixth sub-race humanity, and His teachings will embrace all to which it is possible for the new sub-race to evolve. Each Avatar must have prepared for Him, and must overshadow, inhabit and work through, a body capable of expressing all the advanced truths needed by the sub-race to which He comes. The characteristic of the new sub-race will be a desire to delve into the deepest mysteries of all truth, hence its Avatar must be capable of expressing the most advanced truths given to any Race or sub-race thus far.

The fundamental object of THE ORDER OF THE 15 is to gather together and prepare those faithful Souls who are ready to make conditions for His manifestation possible.

The one rule must be applied to all, namely, "By their fruits ye shall know them." No one can study the pure teachings of the Bab or observe his blameless life and his Christ-like influence and not know that he has The Christ abiding in him.

> "Have I reached that point where I am ready for personal instruction? Am I ready to come into personal touch with the Masters of Wisdom? What directions can you give for forming such contact?"

The way in which a pupil is brought into personal touch with the Masters of Wisdom is firstly, as we state in our circulars, "It will be ONLY THROUGH YOUR OWN INDIVIDUAL EFFORT, your attitude of Soul, and the character of your life that will enable YOU TO PLACE YOURSELF in personal, conscious touch with the Masters. IT DEPENDS UPON NO PERSONALITY BUT YOUR OWN." And secondly, until this conscious touch has been made, you may come into personal touch by correspondence with the Order. For whenever a pupil writes, in singleness of purpose and with a heart-cry for help and enlightenment, the letter sent him in reply is dictated by a Master of Wisdom. Often the application of the letter thus transmitted is not understood by the Agents, for they may not understand the circumstances of the pupil, but, nevertheless, the pupil can see the application of the message. Often, too, the letters are beyond the full comprehension of the pupil unless he studies and meditates upon them. That is, the intuition of the pupil is not sufficiently awakened to perceive under the words the answer to his real need. And since, as it frequently happens, the pupil has his own ideas of what he needs, while the Master takes quite a different view of the situation, it is, in reality, a severe test to the pupil and he often fails to pass it, being unable to recognize the Master's words. Thus the pupil wonders why he has not come into personal touch, as he understands it, and perhaps accuses the Order of misrepresentation. But there is no claim made in the letters that they are dictated by a Master of Wisdom. They are signed by the Secretary who says that he is "directed by the Teacher of the Order to say," leaving it to the pupil to accept it as from a Master or from the human brain of the Secretary, as his intuition directs.

If, however, the pupil recognizes something more than mere human wisdom in the letters and welcomes the Master's words, it is seldom long ere he or she is in interior, personal communication with the Master who dictated the letter. Indeed, many of the more advanced pupils receive the answers to their questions before they have finished writing them to the Secretary and the latter's letter merely confirms what they had received interiorly. . . .

You are ready for personal help when you can recognize and accept the instruction when it comes. Such personal help cannot be withheld when the demand is made; but it never flatters the pupil. On this account the pupil often thinks that the Master does not appreciate him at his true worth, that is, at his own estimation of himself; for the Master gives what is most needed rather than what is most wanted. . . .

As to directions for forming such interior contact, my son, there are no directions that anyone could give you unless your own intuition can speak. If you have formed a conception of a mysterious interview with some wonderful Being whose presence will send thrills down your spine and who will confer upon you some mysterious power that you can carry with you henceforth and proclaim to the world "I am holier than thou, for I have met the Master," then we say, most emphatically, that all the force and power of the great Lodge of Masters would be set in motion to prevent such a catastrophe. Such a thing has never occurred, and never will occur. . . .

The whole thing, in a nut-shell, is that no pupil is left without the help and instruction needed for his advance. At certain stages, life alone can give you this; in other cases there are books and earthly teachers who can give the Soul all that it needs for a certain step in its growth. But when the pupil has culled all the lessons to be learned in these ways; when life no longer teaches, because its simpler lessons have been learned and an interpreter is needed for its mysteries; when books and earthly teachings seem like dry husks, and the Soul cries out for more food, IT MUST BE FED; for this is The Law. Then there begins to come to him something closer, generally as a still small voice, as a dream, vision or distinct impression. If he listens and follows these leadings he will find them confirmed and work out in his life and become steps on The Path, until, finally, he finds himself confronted, not with a mysterious personage, but in close, familiar communion with an Intelligence whom he has learned to love and trust. Only when this interior communion is established can the pupil come face to face with his Guru. Of course this will take place upon the inner planes, but long ere this he will be carefully instructed as to the necessary steps, the necessary cautions to be observed; will be told how to recognize and treat false teachers and false teachings. . . .

The requisite preparation for such close, personal contact is a sincere and loving heart, a child-like confidence and trust, and a willingness to sit at the Master's feet and be taught, rather than to afford an opportunity for the pupil to tell the Secretary how much human wisdom he has obtained. That is, he must be willing to listen to and study and meditate upon the teachings received, no matter how hidden the meaning may at first appear and no matter how opposed to his former ideas and conceptions. All must be carefully weighed and pondered and such as appeal to the pupil as true and right accepted, that is, those that stand the test of the Law of Love and Life. . . .

PART II

CONCERNING THE ORDER OF THE 15

"For my part, having given the greater part of my life to the study and analysis of facts, I would rather be the author of the tritest homily, or the baldest poem, that inculcated that imperishable essence of the soul to which I have neither scalpel nor probe, than be the founder of the subtlest school, or the framer of the loftiest verse, that robbed my fellow-men of their faith in a spirit that eludes the dissecting knife, in a being that escapes the grave-digger." Bulwer-Lytton, A STRANGE STORY.

April 9th, 1908.

"I note that it is stated that the Teachers of the Order will remain hidden. One would naturally wish to know on what authority the contemplated teachings, and the predictions mentioned, are given. However, I suppose that the instruction given will soon show in itself its source. On the other hand, I, in common with others to whom I have shown your circulars, would like, if possible, some more definite information as to the organizers of this movement—the physical plane organizers, if the others must remain hidden."

We are truly sorry that we cannot comply with your request as to the personality of the organizers of this Order. All we can say is that it is a direct outpouring of The Lodge force, and the agents through whom it is manifesting are of no more importance, from the standpoint of the teachings, than would be the pipe through which a stream of pure water was led into a parched and thirsty land. Those who are athirst for the living waters will drink; those who are satisfied with that which is at their disposal will pass it by. Only the thirsty appreciate water.

If a history of the personalities were set forth, with photographs, names, etc., of what avail would it be? Would it make the message any more satisfying? Would it make truth any more true? Or would it, as has always happened heretofore, tend to detract from the teachings? Those who had a personal leaning toward the agent would cling to the personality, excusing every eccentricity and perhaps following some personal bias or weakness, and would waste many words and much force in defending such a personality. Such an attitude has heretofore put many temptations in the path of agents, and has even made them unfit instruments for The Lodge to use. On the other hand, all who did not altogether admire the personality of the agent would have a target at which to throw stones. To them all the teachings would be tainted by the personality of the agent. This, and much more, has been the sad experience of all past attempts to give out The Lodge teachings. Humanity has proved, most conclusively, that it is not yet ready to be trusted with a knowledge of the personality of the agent. Therefore, in sorrow, the Masters of Wisdom have taken away from them the gift which, like children, they have shown their utter inability to appreciate. The Karma ignorantly incurred in the past by the treatment of former agents of The Lodge is to be spared humanity this time. As each individual grows into touch with this work on the soul plane, and displays a right appreciation of the sacrifice made by such agents, and ability to judge the matter impartially and apart from personality, the knowledge may be given them.

You are quite right in thinking that the teachings are themselves their own authority; for if they did not indicate their source no amount of specious claiming on the part of the agents would avail. "If this work be of men, it will come to naught; but if it be of God, ye cannot overthrow it; lest haply ye be found even to fight against God."

At present we can only say that this Movement is a modern prophet without the walls of the city, crying, "Prepare ye the way of the Lord, make his paths straight." It is a modern "Voice of one crying in the wilderness, Repent ye: for the kingdom of heaven is at hand." If that voice finds an echo in your heart follow it; if not, go your way in peace, for your time is not yet come.

June 8th, 1908.

"I note what you say about organizations. I am so glad we can be in the Order of the 15 without being buried within its folds; that we can have its air and its vibrations yet be free. O, that word free means so much to me!"

All real cosmic Orders will aid toward the individualization of freedom. Anything which engulfs you and smothers out all natural growth must be unnatural, hence of man. God works always on broad lines leading to freedom. The true lesson of universal brotherhood and freedom and the oneness of all creation can never be learned except as nature demonstrates the lesson, i.e., each growing thing after its own kind without interference, yet each and all attaining perfection through the same forces—sun, air, earth and water. The oak and the violet at its root, each from the selfsame soil, and in the same environment, attain to an individualized perfection; each adds its quota to the one perfect picture. And the oak does not continually reproach the violet because it does not try to be an oak. The Japanese, through so-called "art," can so dwarf and pervert nature that the oak can grow in a pot no larger than that required for the violet, and this is what many man-made movements are attempting to do with the human oak.

April 27th, 1908.

"I am a Theosophist and would like further information regarding your Order."

Many sincere Theosophists have questioned our Movement by asking why, since it comes direct from The Lodge, it is not given out through the already established channels. We do not desire to have it understood that the formation of this new channel is a reflection upon or a criticism of those organizations; for they all have their particular work. The work of this Order, however, is something quite different, i.e., the interpretation of the teachings of the Master Jesus and the giving of the help required by each Soul after it has reached a certain point of development where the teachings given out to the mass of students as a whole no longer meet its needs. This cannot be done by organizations that are bound by general rules; for their fundamental principle is that all must fare alike and take such general instructions as can be given without regard to the needs of individual pupils. If you will carefully study the lesson on DEGREES AND ORDERS you will understand why such laws and rules are necessary for such organizations, and from their standpoint, are right and proper. They must follow their instructions from The Lodge; for those are laws given to all organizations working on the negative side of the cross. Hence they must follow the negative law, i.e., advance can only be made collectively and all must fare alike as to instruction. THE ORDER OF THE 15, however, as you will see from that lesson, is on the positive side of the cross, and is put forth to aid those who need PERSONAL instruction; those who have reached a point where they can come into personal touch with the Masters of Wisdom interiorly, yet who need instruction and direction in forming such contact. We do not aim to supplant the. . . . , but should supplement their work in greatest harmony; for their teachings are the basis upon which we build and which we require from our pupils. This is the Law: Only he who asks can receive, because the asking opens the doors through which help can come.

May 4th, 1908.

"I very gladly ask to study with you, but in fairness I must say that I am old and sick and poor, and will not consider myself aggrieved if classed as ineligible."

We are most happy to welcome you into our Order. We welcome the "old and sick and poor" and those who are heart-hungry for love and sympathy. Hear ye not the voice of the Master saying, "Blessed are the poor in spirit: for theirs is the kingdom of heaven"? Yea, blessed are the sick; for they shall be healed. Blessed are the old; for they have garnered the wisdom of earth and are nearing the very hour when the Lord shall walk in the garden with them in the cool of the day. Whosoever sends out a cry of heartfelt, loving desire shall be heard and shall meet Him face to face. We are only too glad of the privilege granted us of sending even a little love and light and joy to you.

Can., Jan. 12th, 1908.
"The temperament which I have earned, and of which I am at present the possessor, demands that certain things shall be clearly explained to me, because in this great country of North America, there are more fakes and frauds in so-called Spiritual organizations than in any other country with which I am acquainted. You will no doubt recognize that to those who are worthy of joining your organization you must reveal as much concerning it as will, with their want of knowledge concerning it, satisfy them that you are what you claim to be."

No doubt if this Movement were a fake or a fraud or some scheme to get money from the credulous, there would be voluminous "proofs" and attestations as to its genuineness, and loud protestations of its power to stand above all other organizations. But as it does not belong to that class we must adhere to the universal rule, the law always followed by The Lodge of Masters, i.e., the one law of creation, growth and evolution: "By their fruits ye shall know them." When a planet is born it does not herald the advent abroad, but goes on its appointed way, following the law of its being, until some earnest investigator, who is watching and seeking, discovers and records it. When a tree blossoms or bears fruit it does not blow a trumpet, but waits patiently until someone finds it, and through his previous knowledge of trees, and through his reasoning power, decides that the blossom is rare and that the fruit, even though hitherto unknown, must necessarily be wholesome. This is The Law: true Wisdom cannot swerve from it.

Every Soul has implanted within it, as an integral principle, the power of intuition, just as every mineral, vegetable and animal has the power of selection or instinct which leads it to follow the lines of evolution best fitted for its growth and perfection, in accord with its environment. This beneficent provision was not denied man—the highest point reached, so far, in the scale of evolution—indeed, it was given him in far greater abundance than to the lower kingdoms. With it was given the power of reason, and free will, that he might, if he would, KNOW or he might, if he would, DOUBT and go astray and waste time—a privilege denied the lower kingdoms.

April 19th, 1908.
"What appealed to me so forcibly in THE ORDER OF THE 15 was its grand, broad foundation and the loving help and recognition it held out to those who were ready. In all my asking before in this line, I had been put off with stones, and no recognition of possible individual preparation or development taken into consideration."

When all candidates are placed upon the same level and no spiritual insight is employed, from a merely earthly standpoint all must pass through the same wearying delays. But no movement can be a heart-help which stamps itself, at the outset, as incapable of discerning inward qualifications. All so called "inner" instructions coming from such a body must, of necessity, be designed to help the general mass rather than individuals. It is but a corroboration of the teaching given in the lesson on DEGREES AND ORDERS that, while true and necessary, nevertheless such teachings belong to the negative side of the cross, where advance comes in a general way for the mass of pupils as a whole and is not especially adapted to individual needs.

March 6th, 1908.
"The question arises whether this Order would give such teachings and training or discipline as would clash with that of the. . . . School?"

The object of the personal instruction in this Order is to help each pupil to come into personal touch with his own Guru or Teacher, and thus receive his instruction in practical occultism at first hand. There are no two persons who need exactly the same help, and for that reason no Soul who had not reached Mastery would dare give such instruction and assume the karmic responsibility for the teachings given. Therefore, when a student is prepared for such instruction the Guru will be ready to give him personal training. But unless the student has awakened his intuition sufficiently to recognize the Master's presence, and has acquired sufficient knowledge of the laws governing such communications, the message will be meaningless; for he will be unable correctly to interpret it. This Movement, then, is the fulfillment of the promise made to the students of the. . . . School, as you will, perhaps, realize later on.

April 15th, 1908.
"I want particularly to know whether membership in THE ORDER OF THE 15 is incompatible with membership in the. . . . School."

As to your inquiry about joining the. . . . School, we assure you that it can make no possible difference to us, except that we hope you will not take obligations that will prevent you from remaining in the Order. This Order, being a real Order of The Lodge, is gathering its members from all organizations and cannot possibly interfere with them. In fact we desire to have our members remain faithful to obligations already assumed and thus infuse The Lodge force into their organizations.

May 15th, 1908.
"I never had any uplifting power like I have received from this order. Your first letter and lesson came direct to the soul. I have learned a lot of mantrams but never one that has done me as much good as the one in the lesson. (The MORNING PRAYER. Ed.). . . . I cannot help the Order as I would like but will send you as much as I can as soon as I can."

We are happy to hear that you have been able to correlate with the force sent you; for it is only those who have something within themselves that is attuned to the special note of truth sounded by this Order who can feel the sympathetic vibrations of the life-force from this Center. We understand your true attitude and your desire to help, and, as you know, love and sympathy are far higher and more lasting helps than money. Still, while humanity is bound on the wheel of the almighty dollar, it is impossible to do anything practical to help it, such as sending out these teachings, without the physical expression of interest which takes the form of financial aid. We know, however, that you will do all you can, and we have no fear of the failure of the work. One way in which you can help is to hold strongly to the thought of financial success for the Movement; for it must place its feet upon the earth plane through earthly means, and every one who recognizes this truth practically, helps more than he can understand.

May 22nd, 1908.
"I am being led into new and wonderful paths as fast as I am able to understand their meaning, but I must KNOW that it IS the leading."

As to your just demand to KNOW if this Movement is the leading you are seeking, we can only say that no embodied entity can answer that question for another. Each Soul must decide for itself that all-important question. If you ask sincerely, in The Silence, for guidance, and if it is the real, sincere cry of the heart for help and light that goes out, verily your Father-in-Heaven who heareth in secret shall reward you openly. Never has a sincere cry for help been sent out in The Silence—where God dwelleth—that was not answered. Just as soon as the demand is truly voiced and put into definite form, yea "Before they call, I will answer; and while they are yet speaking, I will hear". The thing to do is to recognize the answer when it comes. That YOU must do for yourself. We can only assure you that we are ready and willing to help you; but our ability to do this depends upon yourself. If you want what we can give, it is yours: if for some reason you need other training for a time, we willingly stand aside and give our time to others who are hungry for the food that is given us by the Masters to break and distribute. It is only five loaves and two small fishes; but to all who sit down and partake it will prove sufficient and satisfying.

Jan. 5th, 1908.

"I certainly 'desire to progress' and therefore shall be glad to hear further concerning that of which the circular treats."

We appreciate your attitude and know the real heart-hunger for growth that is almost fearful lest the proffered food prove to be a stone. Only your own intuition can help you. The table is spread; the garment is ready, and we invite you to the feast. Yea, we welcome you; for we know that hunger which nothing but spiritual food can satisfy. How well we understand the weary disappointment and the cry of your heart, "How long, O Lord? How long?" No longer, my son, than you yourself hold back. Your Father's hand reaches out toward you; a complete happiness and satisfaction is yours for the picking up. "Ask and ye shall receive, seek and ye shall find." There is no death but disappointment and lost ideals. Breathe life into your ideals, new life and hope. Set them once more upon the pedestal and determine that they shall be imbued with life. Nothing is lost but the mere husk of an ideal; the germ is still there, only waiting for the breath of love to bring it forth in new and glorious garments, fit for the wedding feast of thy Soul.

Jan. 16th, 1908.

"I have not been ready to join organizations or movements for fear that they might not be what I needed."

As to your fear that you are wrong in entering this Order, that all depends upon your attitude. There is always one way, and one teacher who can best help each Soul. The Soul knows intuitively, or can know if it will listen, just who can help and just what way is best. There is no one way for all. Each has peculiar affinitizations which in past lives have laid down the lines over which it is easier for helpful force to be drawn. The injunction, "Know thyself" included this point, i.e., to know intuitively what is helpful and to follow that leading independently of what any other may think or say; for what is the correct line for you may be all wrong for your neighbour. Your letter rings true and sincere, and such an earnest call for help never remains unanswered.

April 9th, 1908.
"I do not know what you mean by contributions unless it is to pay for the lessons."

A thing that costs you nothing is valued at nothing. Just in proportion to the real love and sacrifice will be the value to your own Soul. In other words, what we love we work for, sacrifice our time and money for. And out of those things, or their inner force, is our character built up. If we value dress, earthly gain, self-indulgence or earthly honors, we work and sacrifice for them, and the inner force that creates the desire grows into our character. And soon we have either a frivolous, miserly, inordinately selfish or ambitious character. If we desire the fruits of the Spirit—love, joy, peace, long-suffering, gentleness, patience and humility—we will exert our every effort for them. And the effort thus put forth will grow into character; for only through effort can we ever gain them.

You do not PAY for the lessons, but you do all you can to help on the work in whatever way you can, making sacrifices of time, money and thought if you love it and really mean to build into your character "the fruits of the Spirit."

June 14th, 1908.
"I have just carefully read the paper on NARCOTICS and approve of it so much that, with your permission, I will publish most of it in the magazine, and give proper credit."

We are glad the paper on NARCOTICS pleases you. None of our lessons aim to be a complete or full treatment of a subject. This is done intentionally, because we wish not only to instruct, but to stimulate the intuition of our pupils and lead them to write for further explanation; for it is the heart-cry—the need of the Soul—that is answered, rather than the words of the letter.

May 28th.

"I desire to know something of how your work is carried on and what the expense of membership is."

The work of this Order is carried on by monthly lessons and by personal correspondence. That is, all students are privileged to write to the Teacher of the Order and ask questions upon points either in the lessons, in the Bible or in any other teachings. They may also write for advice in regard to their spiritual growth, or whenever they are in trouble and need help and sympathy. Such letters form a direct line of communication over which the helpful forces from this Center can flow continually. . . .

This Movement is supported entirely by voluntary contributions; for no true spiritual teachings can be bought for a price, nor can they be withheld from any sincere seeker who is ready for them.

PART III

PRAYER

"Do you believe that if there really did not exist that tie between Man and his Maker,—that link between life here and life hereafter which is found in what we call Soul, alone,—that wherever you look through the universe, you would behold a child at prayer? Nature inculcates nothing that is superfluous. Nature does not impel the leviathan or the lion, the eagle or the moth, to pray; she impels only man. Why? Because man only has a Soul, and Soul seeks to commune with the Everlasting, as a fountain struggles up to its source." Bulwer-Lytton, in A STRANGE STORY.

"Prayer is an ennobling action when it is an intense feeling, an ardent desire rushing forth from our very heart for the good of other people, and when entirely detached from any selfish personal object; the craving for a beyond is natural and holy in man, but on condition of sharing that bliss with others." Blavatsky, THE SECRET DOCTRINE, Vol. III.

May 22nd, 1908.

"Though the daily petition for physical and spiritual sustenance may be well adapted for those developed to no higher point than the anthropomorphic idea of Deity, it seems to me that, once the consciousness is reached, even if faint and imperfect, that Love and Power are our divine inheritance; ours at the mere desire and will to use them (aright) for the proper reflection upon all other life in full measure, of love and wisdom received by us, is not the cultivation of purity in love and desire—next on the program? Thus while my own children, as infants, expressed their wants or needs, so soon as a consciousness of our relationship was established, the necessity for such expression ceased. (How much sooner had I been omniscient!) So too, our intercourse is one of mutual love; even though mingled with discipline and obedience not one of petitions and favors—this is for masters and slaves."

Your idea of prayer is correct as far as it goes; but it applies only to prayer as generally understood and practiced. There is but one universal Law governing all manifestations of life, from molecule to cosmos, and this works with mathematical precision through foreordained channels. Hence to pray for (get) anything you must obey the Law and seek and expect to get only in accordance with the Law through these natural channels. The Infinite Spirit, manifesting as Father-Mother-Love, as it correlates with matter must, of necessity, work with the Law; for Love is the fulfilling of the Law. Matter, being inert and dense, is opposed to Spirit in that the finer vibrations of Spirit find it difficult to set the comparatively inert matter into harmonious vibration, and as each is at an opposite pole there can be no direct contact the one with the other. Communication between the two must follow the regular, lawful channels. It is here that prayer, in its true conception, comes in. True prayer or spiritual aspiration is simply a correlating of the brain and physical consciousness with the spiritual, thus creating a natural channel of communication through which the spiritual force can flow. In other words, it is closing the circuit. The Will, a desire for spiritual gifts, and a constant attitude of devotion are the proper channels; but words, meditation and a recognition of the end to be attained, are steps leading to the opening of them.

Prayer is a channel leading to the attainment of the fixed purpose (desire for spiritual gifts); and prayer, Will and spiritual desire are steps necessary for those to follow who have not attained that perfect control over the whole life,—mind, emotions and purpose which they may ultimately attain. Those who have attained can well dispense with prayer; but not those who are still striving. Prayer is the Jacob's ladder, one end resting on earth, the other reaching into heaven. If you have climbed to the top of the ladder you no longer have need of it; but it would be cruel to cut away the ladder by which you had climbed when so many eager Souls are clinging to its rungs.

When your sons and daughters were young you expected them to ask for what they thought necessary, even though you in your wisdom did not grant it; but when they had grown to the age of discretion you were content that they should hold an attitude of respectful love and obedience. Until you have attained to YOUR Father's stature in spiritual growth He expects you to ask for what you think necessary, even though He in His Wisdom does not grant it. Prayer is but the asking.

To pray for assistance is, if rightly understood, merely to recognize the inflowing of Divine Love and to struggle to make a place for it. To ask for guidance is but to take hold of the power of Divinity as a little child grasps its father's hand. The child does not say, "Father, give me bread and clothing and houseroom;" for all that is its birthright; but it is quite right to come to its father with its difficulties, its lessons and its little tumbles and bruises and ask for sympathy and help. Altho the child must fight its own way through life you would be a cruel father to refuse a helpful talk if it poured into your ears a tale of difficulty and discouragement, or to refuse sympathy when it was bruised or wounded.

A most erroneous idea of Omniscience prevails. Consider it as perfect Law. Omniscience is All-knowing, and expresses itself perfectly in all minutia, even though we may not recognize that they are perfect expressions of the conditions. To become one with The Law is to have fulfilled it. Jesus came not to destroy, but to fulfill it through the power of The Christ.

March 20th, 1909.

"Healing prayer can be used, with the sanction of the higher nature, only as a preventive of further mistakes. . . . To make the cure of disease the object of prayer is a degradation of this high power."

Prayer, meditation and YOGA are all the same thing, the names differing according to the country you are in. But, my son, I wish to call your attention to a grave misconception which you, in company with many other students, have fallen. Evil Karma is not punishment, neither is it fatality. It is the result of inharmony—a something wrong—a law broken that must be adjusted. And until such adjustment is made more or less suffering must be experienced. It is like a splinter in a tender spot. The spot will fester until the splinter is removed, but would you think it wise to allow the spot to fester until by the sloughing of the surrounding tissues the splinter was eliminated? Or would a wise physician use his higher powers (his trained intelligence) to remove the splinter at once and allow the spot to heal? Again, a wheel has become flattened on one side and runs with great friction and jarring, throwing out of gear all parts of the engine. This, no doubt, is bad Karma from bad usage; but the engineer is fully justified in using his higher powers to have the defect remedied at once. Thus it is with the HEALING PRAYER[1] as we give it to you. The earnest repetition of it, with an effort to grasp its real significance, arouses in the consciousness a realization of what is wrong. You recognize the Divine Creative Force of Love—The Christ Power—and the instant such a recognition is made the splinter is removed, the defective machine repaired and atonement is made; for The Christ has spoken, "Go and sin no more."

Much that is called prayer is but selfish sanctimoniousness glazed over. To make the cure of a condition the object without a recognition of The Law, or to debase the force for personal ends, especially to get money through the gullibility of the weak and suffering, IS NOT PRAYER AT ALL, and therefore does not enter into the discussion.

April 9th, 1908.

"The prayer on HEALING sent last month and the MORNING PRAYER[2] for this month seem to me to be two extremes of thought, one making life here automatic, the other assuming too much individual power. . . . When I was confronted during the day with two aged women, both homeless, and I absolutely had not a place to send them but the almshouse, the words that I had uttered in the morning, 'I can conquer all that comes to me today,' seemed to grin at me in mockery. . . . The effect of the above mentioned prayers would probably cause either complete self-depreciation, or excessive self-appreciation."

All manifestations of life, from molecule to cosmos, are expressed in a circle. If you will let your mind dwell on this

---

[1] See Appendix.
[2] See Appendix.

fact for a moment you will, in fact must, admit that a circle has no beginning and no end, hence no extremes. "Extremes meet," is an aphorism of daily life, and like all such is founded on a rock of spiritual truth. The two prayers you are troubled about stand as examples of this underlying principle; self depreciation from the viewpoint of the lower, personal self; self appreciation from the outlook of the Real Self. Both are true and the force from each flows eternally round and round the circle of manifestation. When one is spending all his energy in work upon the outer rim of the circle as you are, it is impossible to see all the way around. So when confronted with earth misery which you are unable to alleviate, discouragement and a feeling of helplessness is inevitable. Could you but for a moment transfer your activities to the center of the circle you would at once realize that the animating force that keeps this circle of manifestation in being comes from the central point and is distributed equally to all parts of the circle—is the One Life. Working from this central point discouragement is impossible; for at once knowledge comes to you that all is well; that they too, the indigent, the helpless and homeless are in the stream; that the great Heart of Love holds them within Its sheltering folds, and that It does not depend upon your personal ability to place them; that your Father-in-Heaven (the Great Creative Force of Love) has already placed them where they must remain UNTIL THEY HAVE LEARNED A NEEDED LESSON. Your compassion and pity for them is but cold and harsh in comparison with the yearning tenderness of the Masters of Compassion—of the Loving Christ, who would not that any perish but that all have eternal life. They know that time and place are but motes in the sunbeam, and They love with enough intensity to wait patiently until the lessons are learned and the sisters, now so poor and ill, can be clothed with His righteousness as with a garment, and sit down with Him at the marriage feast.

This does not at all decry the necessity for outer work—caring for the desolate ones, "For in as much as ye have done it unto one of the least of these ye have done it unto me." But it does mean that you are to "Work as those work who are ambitious" to lift all the world into better physical conditions, yet you are to "Kill out ambition" and know that all is well. If you have done your best let it rest there. Be strong enough to stand aside and see the workings of the Lord (The Law) and like a little child say "Thy will be done" knowing that the will is to emancipate all from sin and sorrow. But the only path is the one that teaches through experience, and there is more joy in heaven over ONE SINNER that repenteth who has learned his lesson—than over ninety and nine just persons who need no repentance—who are satisfied.

The Shining Ones are all the time creating and building for each and every Soul the immortal habitation (spiritual body) in which that Soul will find ultimate liberation, and if the material out of which that body must be built can only be obtained by tearing to pieces and destroying old earthly habitations (physical bodies) in which the personality has become entangled, They will not hesitate to tear down and destroy. At the end of it all when the lessons are learned and the Soul sits down at the Father's table—do you think a residence of a few short, mortal years in an almshouse will in any way detract from their joy?

PART IV

THE ASTRAL PLANE

"Thou canst not call that madness of which thou art proved to know nothing." Tertullian, APOLOGY.

"The astral influences are invisible, but they act upon man, unless he knows how to protect himself against them. Heat and light are intangible and incorporeal; nevertheless, they act upon man, and the same takes place with other invisible influences." Paracelsus.

April 28th, 1908.
"What IS the astral plane? Is it a place or locality in any sense at all? With all the evidence of the substantiality of the astral plane, when we try to prove things it at once becomes unsubstantial. I can find no landmarks; I cannot even prove whether the beings are external to ourselves or are creations of our own brain, made of the same stuff as are our thoughts—dramatizations of our thoughts—yet this solution does not seem true when checked up by all the facts. What then is real?"

The astral plane is not a place or locality, but a state or condition. To quote from one author: "It cannot be measured in three dimensions, and yet it is capable of measurement by degrees in the scale of vibrations. These states or degrees of vibrations interpenetrate each other without interference, in which peculiarity they have correspondence or analogies in physical phenomena. For instance, a dozen or more currents of electricity may pass along the same wire, at the same time, without interfering with each other, and may then register each on its special instrument, providing that the rate of tension or vibration be different in each case."

The only reality is spiritual consciousness, the One Life; all else is but varying degrees of expression of the One Life. These expressions are cognizable through vibrations affecting organs attuned to receive them. Hence the densest matter or slowest vibration is the physical expression of consciousness, and we are apt to call this REALITY when in fact it is the least real, because least permanent, of all. Try to realize that what appears to you as real is but the greatly slowed down vibrations of the One Life, matter being but retarded motion and in truth ever changing, transitory and evanescent. This is easily proven, for if the experience of merely holding a little paper of a certain drug to your head, as you describe, could so change the rate of vibration of the molecules of your sense organs that they not longer responded to the vibrations of physical matter (for you it no longer existed), but quickened their rate until you were responding to the vibrations of a different world just as real to you then as the physical was, you have proved the matter in your own experience. If you will think this simple example over we feel sure you will understand, in a way that no number of words could tell you, just where the astral world is, and also who and what are its denizens. It is simply the next higher note in the scale of vibration, and its entities are those whose bodies vibrate in harmony with that note. Their senses respond to those rates as readily as yours do to those of this plane, and hence it is just as real to them as this is to you. Therefore, the astral world is around and within you, interpenetrating the physical. The different parts of you—astral, mental, spiritual bodies etc.,—each function upon its own plane. That is, your astral body is now and all the time functioning upon the astral plane, while the higher principles, which connect you with the key-note of your existence and vibrate to its rate, are in the spiritual realm. Your experiences vary with the plane or state of consciousness in which the Ego is functioning. The dense particles of your physical brain vibrate to the rates of the physical and ordinarily confine your consciousness to that plane. But you, yourself, have proven how easy it is to transfer your consciousness and respond to the vibrations of other planes. The path is not a public highway, but is, nevertheless, a well trodden one and easily found by those who know.

All that exists is substance, but in different rates of vibration. One is no more real than the other; for with whatever rate your consciousness is vibrating that rate is real as long as the consciousness functions there. Persons who function consciously in the astral—such functioning being possible because they have dropped their denser instruments—taken off their overcoats, as it were—are just men and women using bodies and senses attuned to that state of matter instead of to the slower, denser, physical matter. Hence, since their range of response to vibration is wider, their limitations are less binding and less hampering. This accounts, too, for their limited knowledge, altho to those still on the earth plane it may seem great. It is unlawful to pass the barrier because the Law of Vibration forbids. Even those upon the astral reach a point where they cannot respond to a still higher rate of vibration and they are limited unless they can receive teachings from those who have reached into still more spiritual vibrations and have gained deeper knowledge. All this, however, can lawfully be accomplished by the true disciple, even while still upon the earth plane. The astral is but the Hall of Learning. Being the nearest to the earth it is the easiest to reach; but man, being essentially a Divine Being, has the power, by uniting his lower mind to his spiritual consciousness—becoming one with his

Father-in-Heaven—to raise his lower vibrations until they are attuned to those of the One Mind or God, and bring back His wisdom through all the realms. This is what we are here to learn, i.e. the powers and possibilities of vibration. "Man know thyself."

All states are real and exist as long as the consciousness holds you there. The Soul, as we have already said, being an expression of the one Great Reality, is always real, and through the real vibrations of mind-substance creates a reality out of whatever it believes, i.e. heaven, hell, etc. That is what your Soul is doing now in regard to the physical plane. From the standpoint of any higher plane physical existence is the most stupid kind of sleep, trance or stupor, i.e. limitation of your Divine powers.

The adjustment of Karma is brought about consciously through spiritual attainment. The Soul in some one life reaches the outermost rim of the Spiral of Life and meets the Saturn force—immobility, stability—and conquers it. Then, in full willingness, desires to go back and pay up all its debts, even those which have remained over from many lives. But while such an one is reaping all sorts of things belonging to his old karmic conditions he, nevertheless, has with him the power of the Conqueror. That is, he KNOWS that these things cannot overcome him; he is above them; he is in them but is not overcome by them; he has become a philosopher and can, like Epictetus, be dragged through the streets in chains and still maintain his peaceful calm.

It is always wrong to force any growth. All steps are necessary. Until you have found the spiritual perfection of each step you cannot pass it; and if you skip one you must come back and take it up later.

March 5th, 1908.

"Does the soul remain in the same state after death or does it pass through various conditions?"

The astral plane is divided into seven degrees or states, called "spheres" by the Spiritualists (most of whom know very little of anything beyond these seven degrees), the lowest of which is very close to the earth. It is in this astral plane—with its seven degrees each divided into seven orders and each order into seven sub-orders—that the Soul works out, or realizes all its earthly desires. If the desires were evil, the experiences will be evil; if the desires were good, the experiences will

The Astral Plane

be good, and the Soul will finally realize just how futile are the merely earthly desires. Some remain on the astral for long periods of time, five hundred years and more, and finally enter the psychic plane (Soul-plane) by dropping the astral body just as the one of flesh was dropped, but generally without the same terror. There they pass through its degrees and orders until they have realized the very highest that they have ever conceived of. That is, every spiritual aspiration has its realization and there is a garnering of the experiences of the earth life. Then there comes a time when the Soul realizes that it has experienced all it knows of spiritual happiness and that there are still heights beyond. It realizes that it must get more experience so that it can gain higher comprehension and higher aspiration. Then its desire for further experience causes it to die to that plane and reincarnate on the earth plane; but not to obtain happiness on earth, for it has realized that spiritual happiness must be born of earthly experience; must be the aroma of self-sacrifice and sorrow. Its only desire is to gain more experience that it may learn higher lessons and so assimilate or gain more spiritual growth and draw nearer to the All through the spiritualizing and redeeming of the atoms composing its various bodies. When this point is reached it chooses its own earth life according to its needs. And from that lofty point the Soul chooses just the conditions which will teach it the lessons it has found itself lacking in. However, it soon forgets this when incarnated in the physical body and forced to express itself through an untrained physical brain, and it has to learn the lessons through sorrow and suffering. Indeed, they would not be lessons if the personality could remember. But the Higher Self (the Soul) always hovers over the personality trying to impress upon it these great truths. We would advise you, if possible, to obtain some Theosophical primers and read as much as you can along the fundamental lines.

June 27th, 1908.

"Why cannot the Agent of this Order communicate with and bring me a message from. . . . who has recently passed out, and tell me if he is satisfied with the condition in which he left his affairs?"

Your letter shows that you have no very clear understanding of the law governing communication with higher planes. The difference between spiritual communication and subjective mediumship is a difference of vibration. The only right way to contact the higher planes is to raise the vibrations of your physical body and its centers until they vibrate in harmony with the key-note of the higher planes, at which pitch "no evil thing can come near thy dwelling." On the one hand—spiritual communication—the psychic, through spiritual living, loving thoughts and helpful actions in many lives, has built into his or her character enough of the Divine Principle of Compassion for all humanity, to raise the vibrations of the physical body, either temporarily or continuously, to the note of spiritual love to which the Masters of Compassion naturally vibrate. As we can only become aware of a thing when some part of our organism responds to its vibrations, the psychic must have the proper development to come into harmony with the spiritual plane ere he can contact the Masters or respond to things which touch upon or vibrate within the octave of Their key-note. And such a psychic would be unable to respond to the vibrations of the lower astral plane except under special conditions which we will explain later.

On the other hand—subjective mediumship—the psychic, through various means, either mentally by stilling the thoughts, or physically by various YOGI practices such as gazing at a crystal, a black spot, or sitting in a constrained position; through breathing exercises and many other still more objectionable practices, has gained the power of stilling the physical vibrations and becoming negative. In such a state the physical atoms, not being held together by the vibratory rhythm to which they naturally respond, slow down and fly off to such an extent that any discarnate entity clothed in atoms of, and vibrating to the note of, the astral plane—which is next to, and in its lower degrees overlaps the earth plane—can gather up and clothe himself in sufficient of the physical atoms thus thrown off to temporarily vibrate to the key-note of the physical plane and become temporarily recognizable on that plane.

In the first instance the whole desire of the psychic is to uplift humanity; he is filled with compassion for the Race and desires to give himself as a willing sacrifice to bring enlightenment to the world. The Teachers and Masters whom he contacts do not see the little individual difficulties, or, if They do, They understand The Law and know that all is working out for the best; that the only Wisdom can really help. Given Wisdom, Love and sustaining help, the disciples can, and indeed must, work out their own personal problems, as Paul says: "Work out your own salvation with fear and trembling." All spiritual communication is uplifting, and the spiritual atoms which the psychic has contacted and drawn into his body will rejuvenate and strengthen the physical, uplift the mental and advance him on The Path of Spiritual Attainment.

In the second instance, by giving up the command over the life forces and throwing open the doors of the sacred centers, the vitality is drawn upon and the atoms thrown off are used to bring to the physical plane the denizens of the astral. These may be pure or vile, and are attracted to the medium in exact ratio to the state of the atoms which he or she gives off during the negative "sitting." If you understand this, and the fact that most of the entities contacted upon the astral plane ARE NOT SPIRITUAL BEINGS, but merely men and women with their most dense and outer garment (the physical body) removed, you will understand the danger of giving yourself up to their use. Since they are using astral senses they can see farther ahead than those on the earth plane, but such advice as they have to give should be taken just as you would take the advice of any earthly friend—subject to your own good judgment and common sense. Usually such entities are interested in the daily life of the sitters, but, if evilly disposed, they can and do often deceive. In no case—unless they are Masters, in which case they will manifest quite differently, as we will explain later—are they any different from the people on earth, except that they are functioning in a body composed of finer matter. They can only come to earth as they left it, i.e. clothed in physical atoms; and the fact that to manifest on the physical plane they must steal physical atoms from the medium and sitters, is proof positive of this. Often their desire is to help alleviate earthly conditions; but their advice, while valuable in many cases, is still in accord with worldly standards. They desire to help their friends out of difficulties, over hard places, and often give advice which helps to make money out of the credulity of their fellow men. This, as you can see, but helps to sink the Race deeper into the mire of earthly affairs. The first is the CONSTRUCTIVE, the second the DESTRUCTIVE method of communication.

You cannot always tell which of the above mentioned methods has been used by the teachings received; for even in subjective mediumship the teaching may be of a highly moral character just as some friend might give you a highly moral address. But no matter who the entity CLAIMS to be, he will NOT be a Master of Wisdom; for no Master of the Right Hand Path ever uses that method. In this case it is not a question of WHAT teachings are given, but HOW they are given.

One absolute test as to which method a psychic is using, and from whence the messages come, is the effect on his physical body. In spiritual communication the psychic is clothed upon by spiritual atoms which self effacement and compassion have drawn to him, and he grows more spiritual. If after the experience his vitality is augmented and a peaceful, happy and vigorous feeling remains, even for days afterward; if life seems fuller, trials easier to bear and love more abundant, you can rest assured that he has risen above earthly things and has been clothed upon by the Spirit, and has brought back lessons for the benefit of humanity. This is the form of communion with the higher planes that should be desired. But do not strive for it; let it come as a natural growth resulting from a life filled with loving, unselfish thoughts and deeds.

In subjective mediumship, however, owing to the loss of physical atoms and vitality, the psychic is depleted and weakened, and soon shows it, not only in bodily health, but also in mental power. His nervous system is enervated, his mentality is dulled and a great stumbling block has been placed in his path. If after communicating, the psychic is exhausted, tired, nervous, cross, fretful and uneasy, even for days, you can rest assured that he has allowed some astral entity to absorb his vitality and contact him by the second and DESTRUCTIVE method.

The exception we mentioned was that there are on the higher planes regular schools of learning, presided over by the Masters of Wisdom. Many persons who pass on with but a slight knowledge of the Wisdom-Religion, but with an intense desire to work for the upliftment of humanity—(quite different from helping their friends in temporal affairs), are brought into such schools and are taught to work consciously on those planes, both gathering together and helping any who, when they pass on, need help of that kind. By the permission of the Masters, and under Their direction, such workers can come into touch with the selected workers of the Masters on the earth plane. They can enter the aura of THE ORDER OF THE 15

The Astral Plane

on earth because both they and the physical plane Agents respond to the same spiritual vibrations from the Masters of the Order. An earthly Agent does not communicate with the astral plane, but is clothed with spiritual atoms, and hence can communicate only with one who responds to the same vibrations, not with any ordinary person who has just passed out. A psychic who has been chosen by the Masters and especially trained to do Their work on earth is carefully guarded. An auric veil is thrown over him which deters discarnate entities from approaching, except by the normal route, i.e. they can be permitted, if it is thought necessary, to transmit a message through one of the before-mentioned trained workers on the astral plane, but in no other way. They cannot come into direct touch unless the Agent is disobedient and perversely throws open the door and scatters physical atoms in sufficient quantity for the disembodied one to create a temporary covering and contact them. In such a case even the Masters cannot protect such an Agent from the consequent evil results.

April 11th, 1908.

"Have often tried to follow the advice of entities on the astral plane who seemed friendly and desirous of helping me, but have generally been misled or they have been unable to fulfill their promises. The mediums themselves have frequently been misled. Why is this?"

In your case we wish to advise you most seriously to keep away from mediums. You, yourself, have all the psychic qualifications necessary, and your centers are already dangerously unguarded to the denizens of the astral plane. Even when such entities are friendly and wish to help you, they are still under the bondage of Karma and are not permitted to do anything for you that would interfere with your working out your lessons. They mean to help you, but are purposely prevented; for if they fulfilled their promises you would once more be enchained in the astral meshes through which it is your present great task to break. That is, YOU must be the Ruler, and must open and shut the doors of your inner centers at your own will. Then such entities will prove themselves your obedient servants and helpers; but they are not for one moment to be permitted to be your guides.

April 11th, 1908.

"That which I have received from you answers all doubts I had. And after re-reading your letter of the 4th instant I could not help exclaiming, 'How wonderful it is that such teachings are offered me'. . . . My occult record and experience contains points that I cannot definitely determine in my own mind as being actual or imaginative. Apparently I have conversed with elementals, with kama-rupas, and with the shells of the multitude and of high statesmen, with Adepts and with the gods of ancient Greece and Rome. Speaking of those I have met from the other side, one day a man asked me to help him out of hades. I said, 'In the name of God arise and pass into a happier world.' And as I watched, the man looked up, his face brightened as he saw a gateway, and with glorified countenance he passed through it. The next day two others applied to me for release. In a few days there was a row of 6 to 12 waiting for me every time I approached the astral plane. Did I do right in helping them?"

Your whole trouble is that you are the reincarnation of an old Atlantean, and are now working out the culminating experiences of all your past incarnations—finishing up odds and ends as it were. If the Soul were obliged to reap all the Karma in one life that it had generated in the last preceding life there would be neither time nor opportunity for progress. Therefore, the Lords of Light hold back a certain percentage from each life, and manipulate the currents of force so that a chance is given the Soul to learn the main lesson of the last earth life and at the same time have an opportunity to gain entirely new experiences. But, before final liberation can come, each Soul must, of its own choice, take up all the accumulated odds and ends of Karma and work them out or redeem them. That is, it must find the germ of good in each experience and discard the husks so that they in their turn may be cast into the great furnace of transmutation (the 8th Sphere) and be purified and evolve into the materials, or world-stuff, from which future globes will be formed.

The earth life you are now living is such a culminating one. Your psychic experiences are due to the Karma made during your Atlantean incarnation. At that time, in common with most of the Race, you abused your psychic power and began to destroy the coverings or oily sheaths that protect the vital centers of the body (see lesson on NARCOTICS), and you have not yet regained complete mastery over them. This is the great task which you must now accomplish. We realize your great need for help, and so are glad that you have frankly told us your exact condition and enabled us to give you exact directions.

Regarding your experience in releasing entities from

hades, all such states are a mere matter of consciousness. From the long continued teachings as to hell and damnation there are many departed Souls who have died in the firm belief that hell was their portion. When they awoke upon the other side they experienced hell; but a hell of their own creation; created by the thought-forms of a lifetime. You, in allowing their belief to influence you, yet desiring to help them, substituted a belief in heaven and found it easy to impose this belief upon them. But it was not in any sense freeing them. It was rather substituting one illusion for another by hypnotic suggestion. Moreover, you attached to your Karma the necessity of final true relief for all whom you thus deluded. The only real way to help such discarnate entities whom you find in bondage to their thought-forms, is to tell them calmly and impressively that hell is only a delusion; that no matter how greatly they have sinned it will all be straightened out later on, as they are able to bear it, BY RESTITUTION ON THE PLANE WHERE THE SIN WAS COMMITTED; that now, while they are excarnate, is the time to rest and gather strength to go on; that they must recognize this and at once seek out the Teachers who are waiting to help them, and from Them learn how to repent and make restitution. Teach them that repentance is turning around and doing the square thing by those whom they have wronged; that no amount of suffering in their self-created hell can do anything but retard their making restitution, and hence their upward journey.

Feb. 5th, 1908.

"What, if anything, of comfort can you offer for the losses to the living of the dead? I am so weary of not KNOWING that it is better with those who are gone beyond. What can you say of it?"

This short period of limitation, mis-called life, is but a veil hiding the Real Life from you. It is as though you tied a bandage over your eyes during a journey and then denied the sunlight and the beautiful landscape. Life is continuous; the consciousness only recedes within. Periodically the outer covering (the physical body) is slipped off just as you would slip off an old garment. The Soul, the Immortal Ego, is the Real Self which clothes itself with various garments suitable to contact the different spheres and states of consciousness. It does this just as you would don different garments for different occasions; a fur coat for winter, a thin one for summer. Slipping off the fur coat does not in any way alter your individuality, even though it does reveal your true appearance more perfectly. You are the same woman whether dressed in a single garment or wrapped in many. So it is with the Real Self. At the time of the so-called death the grossest and most hampering garment, comparable to the fur coat, is slipped off and the consciousness is expanded and freer just as you are freer with your fur coat off. You, when wrapped in your fleshly garments, are perhaps blind to the more etheric and radiant garment, because of the thickness of the outer; but your loved ones know you as you are. Every effort you make to advance spiritually helps them more than it does you, and they in turn help you. For instance, a truth that might be very hard for you to grasp would be quickly grasped by one who was near you yet unhampered by a fleshly body. He in turn would bring all his loving force to bear to help you to understand.

When persons pass from the earth life their character is in no way different. They know just as much as they did before and no more. The chief difference is that they are in a different environment where their faculties of perception are keener. For instance, they can sense thought, while those on earth have to wait for words. They can see within as well as without, and can transport themselves from place to place by the power of thought. Therefore you can well understand that, passing into this new phase of life with all the love of their hearts concentrated on a loved one still on earth, they would not desire to pass farther on into higher spheres, but would stay close to the one they loved. And on the astral plane there are Masters whose pleasure it is to teach all who desire to learn, just as They teach those who still remain on earth.

April 11th, 1908.

"I used to have explosions in my brain, some very violent, but know of no damage from them. Very heavy tremors have, and still occasionally run through my body, shaking it subjectively just as a heavy earthquake would shake the physical body. Have had an exudation of vapor or smoke from a point at the end of my spine, that blackened the chairs I sat on. Vapor or mist exuded from my eyes so much as to moisten a sheet of paper held an inch away. At times the vapor exuded from my wrists. Can you explain it?"

The mist proceeding from the centers of your body is a danger signal, quite as dangerous as smoke coming from a rapidly revolving axle. The tremors you mention are merely contacts with the denizens of the astral. Always challenge them. Ask them what they want. Say, "If you come for help I wish you well, but at present I must guard and protect my own body, hence Begone! Work out your own salvation." If a Master should come to you you will at once know it by the wave of love and joy that surrounds you. But remember that insanity stands very close to undue or abnormal development, and that it is the Masters who are holding you back. They desire that you should go slow until you can gain mastery over your centers; for it is just such tangled ends of mis-applied psychicism that you have now to untangle. It means victory or death, or say instead of death, another long, long cycle of rehabiliment extending into the next manvantara. Your Father-in-heaven hath need of you NOW. The time of times is at hand, and you are chosen to be a Light Bearer. Hold high your light and be diligent. Clear away the rubbish that the light may shine unimpeded.

March 4th, 1908.
"I rejoice that admission and instruction in the Order. . . . is a possibility for me. . . . It is a matter of joy to me to come in touch with an organization which is conducted on purely impersonal lines. The necessity for this has been impressing itself upon me for many years. . . . How can we protect ourselves on the astral plane?"

You must now understand, thoroughly and practically, that nothing can enter your aura, either asleep or awake, without your consent. Therefore, impress it firmly upon your subconscious mind that whenever ANY entity, on any plane, comes to you you are ALWAYS to challenge it. Ask, Who are you? Are you black or white? What do you want with me? If you are not here for my good I will have nothing to do with you. If they hesitate or do not reply to any of your questions INSIST that they do. Demand reply "In the name of The Christ." It is a law on the astral that all such fearless questions must be answered truthfully; but you must DEMAND the truth. Anyone connected with The Great White Lodge will be glad to respond to such challenges and you will feel a thrill of joy and confidence at the reply. Any others must show their real natures or disappear.

April 11th, 1908.
"It appears to me that I have an accumulated inheritance of secret devils among which stand out prominently a hasty temper, a sharp tongue, intellectual pride, and last but not least, lascivious thoughts."

Hold the thought persistently in mind that the devils you speak of are the children of your own creation; not mere characteristics, but really created entities upon the mental and astral planes, entities which you through many lives have created. Being your very own you must master them. But mastery does not mean annihilation; for all that is has within it a germ of good as well as evil, and this germ is expressed according to the use that is made of it. In fact evil is but the shadow of good. It is the work, and the first step, of every earnest seeker after freedom to take stock, as you have done, of just what he has created out of the God-power of creative force given him "in the beginning" as his most precious possession.

When you have taken such stock, realize that these things are yours to use, the weapons with which you must fight, the forces and materials out of which you must build up your immortal habitation. Realize that nothing once created can ever thereafter cease to be; also that the redemption of all through the power of The Christ must be accomplished. It is this that gives true individuality to each one; for while all are one, yet each makes an individual expression of the One Life by creating through the power of his life-force. Since all your creations must be redeemed by their creator all sorts of experiences are garnered and stored up for the One Life.

A hasty temper is like a fire; put it in a furnace and it will generate steam or force that will run machinery and accomplish a great work for the world. A sharp tongue, controlled, will be a weapon that can fearlessly cut the evil from the good; its ruler is love. Intellectual pride is a dangerous master, but a wonderfully efficient servant. Wed it to humility and let love bless the union. Lascivious thoughts are astral lust-bodies created by the mis-application of the physical creative fluid; for remember that that fluid always creates, if not upon the physical plane (physical bodies) then upon the astral, following out the desires and lusts of the creator. (See lesson on PURITY.) Learn the holiness and the sacredness of the sex forces, and send out thoughts of love and purity that will conquer and transmute these creatures of lust, and take their place as helpers rather than hinderers.

Keep on praying; but consciously assert your power, through your divine heritage, to hold all your d-evils subject to you. Chain them and put them to work under the lash of your purified Will until they can be transmuted and redeemed by you, through the power of The Christ.

May 15th, 1908.

"My psychic experiences lately have been quite frequent. My father-in-law who has been called out of the body seems to come back and he and I always seem to have a lot of trouble. He seems bound to push his way into my presence causing trouble. This happens at night and my brother-in-law that was called to pass on in February last comes and plays the same kind of pranks to scare children that he did when on earth. What shall I do?"

You must learn to protect yourself on the astral plane. This is quite as necessary, or more so, than on the earth plane. Think of yourself as one with a glorious Father-in-heaven who is constantly shedding over you a radiant light. This light is a force or flame coming from above, or rather from within your own heart (the lamp). But there must be the oil of love and the wick of truth and confidence and trust, so the light may shine forth in the darkness and make a ring of light and force around you. As far as the light can send forth its rays you are surrounded by a protective aura, and no entity can penetrate within this ring unless you open a door. Keep your doors diligently; open them only to go forth carrying blessing and help to all who need, but shut them tight against any who would enter to desecrate the Holy Temple. Hold fast to the idea that you desire nothing but Divine Wisdom and will admit nothing but Spiritual Light. Study carefully the lesson on NARCOTICS, ALCOHOL AND PSYCHISM which we are sending you.

April 11th, 1908.

"Something attacked me in three different houses, here and in. . . . Would feel a weight on my chest as of a large animal. With a sense of distrust I tried to mentally oppose it, only to find that my brain power was clogged, nor could I open my eyes. After a struggle lasting apparently several minutes I was able to clearly formulate my thought. Then the ill presence would disappear. This had happened a number of times, when one morning. . . . I had barely closed my eyes when the animal pounced upon me. I decided instead of resisting to lie still and see what it would do. According to its feel I judged it to be a cross between a Newfoundland, a bear and a wolf. It wriggled its paws under my back and lifted me clear off the bed. I thought it was then time to resist, and a terrific mental encounter followed. Finally it uttered a horrible growl of disappointment, USING MY VOCAL ORGANS, relaxed its hold and I dropped to the bed with a heavy thud. . . . Before that I several times woke to find my body and arms covered with cuts and scratches which would soon scab over and scale off. What is the explanation of these attacks?"

The beast you mention is directly connected with your old Atlantean incarnation. In those days the Race, having their psychic faculties fully developed (these faculties came first and only later, through misuse, hardened into the present limited physical faculties), used them to enslave all forms of life below them. They had beasts larger and quite different from any now known on the earth plane. These beasts were controlled by hypnotic power and were forced to act as servants and slaves. As the mind of the human being was imposed upon the animal consciousness, the animal became an anomaly, neither beast nor man. On this account they could not proceed normally with their evolution through the animal kingdom, but must wait, outside as it were, attached to the person who was responsible for their unnatural state until, through the power of awakened Will on the part of their sponsor, such beasts are released.

Such astral beasts from time to time send out emanations as it were, which incarnate on the physical plane as animals. These animals would, of course, be of extraordinary sagacity; for, unlike normal animals, they would have something akin to a Higher Self in the astral beast from which they emanated, and they would naturally attach themselves to the human being who was responsible for the astral beast. That is, through these animal expressions the astral beast is able to gain the evolution of its purely animal instincts; but it must remain in the astral and wait for the man to evolve its more than animal wisdom. Much depends upon the treatment you give such animal emanations. No doubt you have had many attach themselves closely to you on earth.

The beasts upon the astral are either ferocious and vindictive or loving and protecting according to the manner in which they were treated in the past. One of the sins for which the ancient Atlantean Race was destroyed was cohabiting with beasts and denying and preventing their normal evolution.

June 16th, 1908.

"While experiencing no 'recoveries' I have seen in part what I have called 'I.' And O the horror of it! I had but a glimpse or two—for although knowing that it was possible to see all, I realized that it was dangerous, in my nervous condition, to try to bear the strain of a full revelation. . . . Since that awful experience my whole outlook and inlook have changed. I see mankind—myself included through different eye-perceptions."

The experience which was so appalling to you was a momentary glimpse of "The Dweller on the Threshold." This is the condensed essence as it were of all the old personalities that you have used in other lives and have not yet conquered, a sort of a composite of all the left-overs from each life. At the time of laying aside the old garment (physical body) there is always a great deal of evil that has not been spiritualized, and this is entitized and remains upon the kama-lokic plane until the Ego who gave it birth grows strong enough to conquer it once for all. It attaches itself to the Ego at each new incarnation and becomes the tempter of the personality—a personal devil to a certain extent, but only because it is something that you have created which is seeking expression through you. It is a personal devil just as the Higher Self may be said to be a personal God.

Before final liberation this monster must be consciously met and conquered, i.e. the evil that is entitized must be redeemed and spiritualized by seeing in oneself the faults that live in this Dweller and overcoming them one by one. It is called "The Dweller on the Threshold" because when one is determined to live a spiritual life this thing stands at the threshold to be redeemed before the neophyte can go on. Very often just before taking an advanced step upward and inward, or passing an inner initiation, this Dweller becomes visible to the disciple. It is dreadful because, being created by yourself, there is an inner conviction that you, like Frankenstein, are looking into the face of a monster of your own creation and you are appalled at the sight of your handiwork. It is only the brave and the steadfast who can look in the face and defy this Dweller, in full consciousness of their power of The Christ to conquer and redeem it. Until redeemed it is ever with you, seen or unseen. If you have ever read Bulwer Lytton's "ZANONI" you will remember that the Dweller was more dangerous when not seen. It is a good thing to see it, for then your courage is stimulated to conquer it. Do not be discouraged; for not only have you a Dweller, but you also have a "Guardian of the Threshold." This is built up or created by you out of all your aspirations and struggles to overcome. Every time you turn your thoughts toward spiritual things you strengthen this Guardian and withdraw life from the Dweller. This is why it fights against your spiritual growth; it is fighting for its life. Every fault faced and overcome adds an arrow to the quiver of your Guardian. This is the meaning of the passage in "LIGHT ON THE PATH" which says: "Stand aside in the coming battle, and though thou fightest be not thou the warrior. Look for the warrior and let him fight in thee. Obey him not as though he were a general, but as though he were thyself, and his spoken words were the utterance of thy secret desires; for he is thyself, yet infinitely wiser and stronger than thyself." The warrior is your higher principles together with the sum total of your aspirations etc. which fights for you. Recognize that the evil is but transitory; that it lives only until you arise in your might, accept it as your own and determine to redeem and transmute the foul dross into pure gold. Remember, nothing is to be killed. "Thou shalt not kill" means more than the surface interpretation generally given to it; for within every evil thing there is the germ of good. Find then that germ, and water it with love and patience until it grows and transforms the evil into good.

You are quite right not to expect or count upon psychic experiences; but when they come meet them boldly and find the lesson in them. Remember always that you have the power of The Christ to conquer everything that comes to you. Use that power and fear not.

March 3rd, 1908.
"Mediums claim to see and talk with those who have been gone as long as 40 years. They are not happy. . . . claim to be 'learning.' Why do not THEY incarnate again?"

Those whom mediums contact who say they have been on the astral plane for a period of forty earth years (a very short period of astral existence) are persons who passed out with no knowledge of the astral plane and with great fear or intense regret at having to leave the earth plane. Moreover, their earth life was probably such that there is now nothing in them to attract them to the Teachers of the astral plane, hence, like so many on the earth plane, they go on and on in ignorance, in spite of the many sources of enlightenment all around them, just as they passed by similar sources while on the earth plane. They are generally those who have centered all their interests on the petty things of earth and who had no realization of a future life. Hence when they find themselves minus a physical body, their interests being wrapped up in earthly concerns, they cannot separate themselves from earth conditions or find interest in anything higher. They hover around their old earth friends and interest themselves in their old earth pursuits. Being able to perceive their earth friends, they are deeply grieved and unhappy because their earth friends do not recognize them, and because their place on earth seems to have been filled and themselves forgotten.

They do not reincarnate because ere they can do so they have a considerable period to pass on the astral and higher planes assimilating the results of the last earth life, and then a period of rest analogous to sleep before they are ready to reincarnate. The best way to help such persons is to impress them with the reality of the plane on which they find themselves and to urge them to seek out those Teachers and Guides who can teach them how to make the best use of their time while there and thus prepare for still higher planes. There are some who refuse to go on until they die to that plane as they did to the earth plane, because there is nothing in them that attracts them toward higher things.

PART V

PHENOMENA

"If anyone think these things incredible, let him keep his opinions to himself, and not contradict those who, by such events, are incited to the study of virtue." Josephus.

June 7th, 1908.

"One evening about nine o'clock I was driving a very gentle team hitched to a good buggy with a good harness. Had been driving most of the day and was near home going up an easy grade in the road at a slow walk, with the traces barely stretched, till I reached the top of the grade, when like a flash of lightning all four traces dropped to the ground, frightened the team which ran away and left me sitting in the buggy surprised. I got the team and found nothing wrong or broken about the harness or buggy. I know that it was utterly impossible for any of the traces to have come unhooked of their own accord. It was a very calm, beautiful moonlight night with not a breath of air stirring. It has always been a mystery to me how this could have occurred without the intervention of some mysterious power from the other world. Can you explain it?"

Your experience with the falling of the traces is what some would call remarkable, but in reality it was only the work of elementals—irresponsible beings in the process of becoming. They can be very mischievous at times, and being without mind of their own, swarm around anyone who gives off enough psychic force for them to appropriate. They are the elements from which human bodies will be built. They have human sub-consciousness, but not self-consciousness, and they therefore obey the thought of humanity as a whole. In the case of their attaching themselves to a human being they obey his thought, even when unexpressed, and are a strong factor in thought power. In your case you were, no doubt, unconsciously or sub-consciously thinking of getting home and unharnessing, and, having very strong mental power, the elemental force of your thought took physical expression and unharnessed then and there. This is the general explanation in most such cases; for if it were the work of any self-conscious entity upon the higher planes it would have had some meaning or reason, either as a warning or to prevent an imminent danger. With you this was not the case; in fact it created danger, since the team ran away.

It is well to be acquainted with the laws of the unseen universe, for man should be the master of ALL conditions. One capable of sending out this force powerfully enough to create a response such as you experienced would, if the power were studied and turned to good, be able to master and command these elemental forces and make them his servants to help him attain betterment for the human race, rather than mischief for himself.

July 21st, 1908.

"On a number of occasions, after deep meditation on religious subjects, I have found myself surrounded by a luminous ether which palpitates with a strange energy unlike anything I have observed in any manifestation of nature."

The luminous ether you speak of is often the astral light. At other times it is the thought-force from the Teachers who are sending into your aura the Light of Wisdom in an effort to awaken in you a responsive vibration that shall make you consciously realize Their presence and grasp Their teachings. . . . The Masters know what lessons They have been trying to impart, but They cannot tell how the lesson has been interpreted by your physical consciousness unless you report what conception you brought back on waking.

March 18th, 1908.

"Yesterday in meditation I challenged a persistent influence within my consciousness, when suddenly with my eyes closed, I saw at quite a distance a figure appear wrapped in a dark mantle with what looked like rays of light extending in all directions around his head. It did not advance or make any movement, and gradually faded away. . . . What you write of the 'ring of force,' the 'Ring-Pass-Not,' is very clear and helpful to me. I have studied it carefully and feel that it is a sure protection of which I gladly avail myself. . . . I shall faithfully apply your instructions in regard to it."

One thing to keep in mind is that no Master will ever enter within the "Ring-Pass-Not" unless especially invited. He may send force to help you, may knock at the door, but He will not enter without your express desire. The law is much like that of the physical plane; for no right minded person will enter the closed door of a private apartment without invitation or permission. In this case no evilly disposed entity can enter the "ring" any more than a thief can enter a securely locked apartment. If this rule were not rigidly followed there would be no privacy on the higher planes. This is the reason for the saying found in the Bible that no busybodies can enter the Kingdom; for while there is the slightest curiosity or desire to pry into another's business one is debarred from functioning on the higher planes. The entity who approached you was not invited to enter, therefore he retired.

May 7th, 1908.

"Why should I be sensitive to elemental forces that may or may not be aware of my existence? Why should I fear them? I am always most uncomfortably sensitive to atmospheric conditions before a storm, but when snow is falling I have a feeling of calmness. Why? Also please tell me about color vision. To me it is divided into color KNOWING and color SEEING, the first being a much higher faculty than the second. The only colors I ever see are those that come in the night just before sleeping. Great soft clouds of beautiful light, mainly blue. Why on earth blue? When as an earth color it does not attract me much."

Sensitive persons are always more or less oppressed with vague fears during a wind storm because the elementals of the air (Sylphs), of all the elementals, act with the greatest malignity toward mankind. While they are on the rampage a sensitive feels their malignant force. The elementals imprisoned in the snow crystals, on the contrary, are kind and benign.

Blue being the color of the mental plane, naturally, when functioning on that plane you see blue—a very intense, beautiful, indigo blue unlike any shade on the physical plane. The "color knowing" of which you speak is commonly classed as the "sixth sense," but it is merely the functioning of one of the five senses on the higher planes, not a new sense. It is by no means spiritual, but simply a faculty developed a little in advance of the general run of human senses. It will be the heritage of the sixth sub-race, and is now beginning to make itself known. That is, we have now reached the point where the fifth and sixth sub-races blend and overlap; for you know there are no hard and fast lines, but, like the colors of the rainbow, one blends into the other.

As to your various psychic sensations, they are quite easily understood. If you could enter into the consciousness of a newly born babe you would find that its physical experiences were very similar. It would be conscious of a bright light, but would not be able to grasp the meaning of it. Forms would come and go like phantoms, and scraps of conversation, probably not understood— altho not necessarily so—would be heard. Colors would be sensed and would have a decided effect upon both feeling and seeing. A babe spends most of its time sleeping, during which it is on the astral plane, with only fleeting periods of physical consciousness—its waking moments. It finds its brain quite unable to grasp the meaning of what goes on around it, and the effort to fix its mind upon anything sends it off to sleep—back to the astral consciousness. You are a babe upon the astral, that is all—quite a precocious one in fact. If you wish to know how to grow up, follow the example of the infant in its various steps toward comprehension of earthly objects.

May 18th, 1908.

"I want to know all I can be given about color. Color has always played a most vital part in my conscious thought life. From earliest childhood everything, words, persons, days, numbers and events have all had their corresponding color by which I knew them better than by any other way."

The innate meaning of everything is expressed in color, tone and form. The form we observe with our physical eyes, the color with the psychic senses. Tone belongs to the creative hierarchy, hence a strong reason for modulating and harmonizing even the tones of the voice. While all color is the natural result or effect of tone, from another point of view it is the result or effect of form. Hence nothing can have a form without a color, nor tone without color, nor either without the other. If you would follow this inspiring line of study, one for which your natural development fits you, you would find all creation an open book. Its alphabet is written in four letters, i.e. form, color, tone and number. Not an herb that grows but proclaims aloud, in unmistakable language, its exact use, power and potency. This is as true of the stars in heaven, in fact of everything in humanity and in the cosmos. Verily, to the eye that can behold and to the ear that can hear there is nothing hid that shall not be revealed.

June 2nd, 1908.

"In my visions landscapes always look perfectly natural; even when everything is in the lights and shadows of flaming yellow, everything is bathed in a glow of yellow light."

Yellow pertains to the soul plane, and a vision tinged with this color should be interpreted as pertaining to the Soul or Ego. Violet is the plane of the spiritual auric envelope, it being blue on the physical plane. It is the highest color and means suffering only when degraded and debased and forced to reflect itself in physical matter. It varies all the way from deep violet described above to pure white, indicating pure, untrammeled Spirit. Orange is the color of the life-force, and according to the degree of its lightening up into golden radiance does it indicate spiritual life, or physical life if there is an interblending of colors.

March 8th, 1908.

"One day not long ago I was walking down Walnut Street when I appeared to be preceded by a purple patch of light. I thought at first it must be an optical illusion, but closing and opening my eyes at intervals and still seeing the light, even with my eyes shut, it made me think it might have some occult significance, hence my mentioning it to you."

The light which you saw was the light of the astral plane, violet being its most prominent color. If it was dark in hue it might have proceeded from a passional element in your own aura; but if it was dark and clear and rich, and a true shade, it would probably represent passion made as holy as earth love could make it. For you know purple is a mixture of red and blue, and it is only by a perfect blending of these two, in purity and love, that gives the highest color of the spectrum violet, at which point the highest attainment of man is reached. Man must follow the path of the pure spectrum colors and create a pure, rich, perfect purple before he can enter into a higher state where violet—which is red purified and enlightened—will prevail.

May 30th, 1908.

"I want to ask for the explanation of much of the electricity that I see. . . . It shows itself as an intense brightness or even sudden contact with a physical object gives me a flash all over."

It may be the result of several causes. The most probable is that you are developing the sense of touch on the astral. If this sense were understood and trained it would make you aware of forces within as well as without. Contact with the aura of an object carelessly touched would be just as tangible as the striking of your body against a hard physical substance as to your physical senses.

PART VI

DREAMS AND VISIONS

"And they said unto him, we have dreamed a dream, and there is no interpreter of it. And Joseph said unto them, Do not interpretations belong to God? tell me them, I pray you." Genesis XL, 8.

"And Pharaoh said unto Joseph, I have dreamed a dream, and there is none that can interpret it:. . . . And Joseph answered Pharaoh, saying, It is not in me; God shall give Pharaoh an answer of peace." Genesis XLI, 14-15.

May 30th, 1908.

"Will the Teacher of the Order help me to a fuller understanding of the very definite psychical experience that has come to me during the last few years?"

We will most gladly help you to an understanding of the psychic experiences you mention; but in order to do this it is necessary that you tell us just what the experiences were. The Masters know just what lessons your Higher Self has been making an effort to impress upon your brain consciousness, but, as in all such cases, the transmission of the higher teaching depends upon how much the lower brain-mind is capable of receiving and translating into physical consciousness. A study of psychology will teach you that the brain-mind can grasp nothing of which the picture, or at least some idea, has not been registered within it by stimuli reaching it through some avenue of perception. Hence, since the language of the spiritual plane is incomprehensible to the mortal mind, the Higher Self has to make use of symbology—in other words, has to make use of pictures of every day events with which the brain-mind is stored—to convey the desired lesson. The consciousness of each Soul is a private book open only to the Higher Self who is giving the instructions. Therefore, while the general character of the lessons may be known, we do not know the particular one given at a particular time. Hence if you will tell us exactly what you were able to remember of any lesson, we will gladly interpret it for you.

This is the explanation of all coherent dreams, as well as signs and omens. Simply some common thing which the brainmind will understand is pictured to you that, by analogy, "As above, so below," you may grasp the underlying divine truth.

Jan. 27th, 1908.

"Sometimes during sleep I seem to comprehend that a message is sent me by another, and at times I feel that I am sending myself a message. . . . "

It would seem that you have brought back with you, in a fragmentary way, impressions from the spiritual plane clothed in physical symbology. However, your impression of having received messages from higher sources is quite correct. You have also given yourself messages; for, during sleep the Higher Self, who is one with the Supreme, is the Captain in Command as it were, and is always trying to impress upon you the teachings that are your birthright. The best way to remember these lessons is to try to identify your lower consciousness with the

Divine in you. Determine that you will become what you really are on the higher planes—a Divine Emanation, of which your lower self is but the instrument, but one which must be tuned up to the key-note of the Divine in order that the necessary lessons may be impressed upon your physical brain. It is very much like wireless telegraphy. The force is sent out, but unless the receiver is attuned to the key-note of the sender, the vibrations cannot be received. The physical must register the Divine, and in doing so it has to make use of the pictures that it finds in the physical brain. This is why you can come into conscious touch with the Masters, or with your Higher Self, only when you have attuned your mind and life to Their plane and can understand Their language; for there must be something upon which to register and a language or means of communication whose meaning you can grasp.

June 17th, 1908.

"Two dreams made a great impression on me. The first one when I was in my native country. . . . happened when I was about 18 years old. I dreamed that I was traveling, traveling on foot through fields and solitary deserted countries through snow and ice. I was tired and footsore and hungry, on each step I stumbled and fell. I was discouraged and despondent yet I tried to keep on moving, going, going without end.

"The second dream I had about 13 years ago when I began to investigate spiritualism. I dreamed that I was introduced, i.e. brought to, Jesus, who sat in a small room bare of any furniture except a plain wooden judge's chair with a straight back, on which He sat all clad in a white robe of ancient style. He was there alone. A man with a flowing beard, bareheaded, clad in ancient apostolic dress, carrying a long staff, brought me before Jesus. But Jesus looked very sternly and would not accept me. . . . The purpose I was brought to Jesus I understood was to be initiated into a secret lodge."

Your first dream was an out-picturing of the very attitude and experiences that you are now passing through. The cold, ice-bound country over which you stumbled so foot-sore and weary, yet with the determination to keep on going, is your present condition. You have stuck doggedly to it in spite of discouragement and it has now brought you to a house of rest where we bid you stay and consider the way you have come, and henceforth walk without stumbling over the hillocks of ice, and draw near to the streams of love that will manifest to you the moment you open your heart to receive them.

Your second dream was also most significant, and in another way warned you of the stumbling blocks which you should avoid. Once more are you brought, by the same guide, into the presence of The Christ for judgment. But this time it is not a mere prefiguring, but an actual working out of the dream. You stand today in that empty Hall of Initiation, empty of everything but your own Soul and your Judge. No failure of another can excuse you. The Judge asks, "Brother, are you ready to stand alone and naked for judgment? What has your own Soul to answer?" The answer is breathlessly awaited.

This Order is the outward manifestation of the secret Lodge into whose outer courts you will enter if you pass your initiation. When the main question is answered all will come about well. You are not forgotten or lost in the icy world, but a hand strong and warm is reaching out to you. Will you take it?

Feb. 27th, 1908.
"I was shown a full moon in the heavens, then three sunrises in succession, but the sun did not fully rise.". . . .

Your vision of the full moon and the sunrises was very significant of the teachings that are promulgated through this Order. The moon symbolizes intuition, also the feminine principle. In order to enter the real ORDER OF THE 15, up to which these lessons lead, you will have to cultivate those principles; for this Order represents the full status of true womanhood. The sun, the orb of day, the Prometheus' Fire, was rising and filling the world with glory, yet the moon (Luna, Queen of Night, the occult or unmanifested side of life) was full and was shining undimmed. The three sunrises while Luna still shown have a deep meaning and refer to a period of time. This, however, is a purely personal matter which you will, no doubt, understand. The whole dream was an effort of your Higher Self to impress upon your brain consciousness some conception of the important era that is now about to dawn for you.

June 18th, 1908.
"One day last summer while resting with eyes closed I had a vision. A bunch of sunflowers encircled by beautiful hands was held out to me. This picture gradually dissolved and violets appeared, surrounded with green leaves."

Sunflowers bring to you the force of the sun. They are also symbolic of faith and trust and steadfastness; for they are always turning a smiling face to the burning sun, no matter how fierce its rays. They exemplify the words of Job, "Though he slay me, yet will I trust him." The violets bring sweet peace and rest and modest content, and a willingness to do the duty that lies nearest at hand in love and patience.

PART VII

HEALTH AND DISEASE

"All diseases, except such as come from mechanical causes, have an invisible origin, and of such sources popular medicine knows very little. . . . There is a great difference between the power that removes the invisible causes of disease, and which is Magic, and that which causes merely external effects to disappear, and which is Psychic, Sorcery and Quackery." Paracelsus.

April 27th, 1908.

"Have arrived at a stage of development where I need the guidance and help of one who knows, and can tell me what to do to correct the suffering. Can neither sit, stand nor lie down, but what I am conscious of pain along the whole length of the spinal cord."

We sympathize with you in your suffering, and desire to help you. Take the HEALING PRAYER[1] as your daily companion. That is, do not merely repeat it; but take it with you in your heart and repeat it word by word, and meditate upon each word until the real meaning and the strength becomes a part of you. Dwell upon it until even the subconsciousness of the cells of your body begin to take up the wonderful vibrations of the healing force, and the Divine Power of Omnipotent Life finds a channel through which it can flow unimpeded in healing streams through all your bodies. First, picture to yourself for at least a day, or longer if you cannot make it a reality in that time, the Master Jesus. Think of Him as a man Who has obtained mastery over physical forces and who especially understands the manipulation of and correlation with the One Life. Think of Him as standing at the head of the great Hierarchy of Healing, all-powerful and full of Wisdom, knowing the lessons of suffering and the necessity of having the body adjust itself to the higher vibrations; knowing that suffering is the result of ignorance as to just how to bring about the readjustment. This readjustment is often learned only after many lives of suffering; but it is a lesson that all must learn. Then think of Him as a loving, tender, helpful Master whose high office and loving desire it is to help His children in making their readjustment; Who is waiting and watching in patience, and in love that passeth understanding, to stretch out His hands to all who cry unto Him aright. THE MERE DESIRE FOR PHYSICAL RELIEF IS NOT ENOUGH. There must be a realization of what pain is and why you suffer. If you cannot find such a realization, then a cry for light and understanding will bring it to you. The cry should not be to take away the pain; but to teach you the lessons of pain. Ask with all your heart and KNOW FULL WELL that the love which suffers with you, knowing that you must conquer through knowledge, is only too eager to help you. Believe that your Father sees you while you are yet a great way off, and goes forth to meet

---

[1] See Appendix

you. The new robe of health and purity is awaiting you, and the feast is spread.

In this way, sentence by sentence, go over the Prayer taking a new sentence each day, and verily, verily when you have grasped the meaning of it all the new life will be yours. But remember that all spiritual force must enter the physical body from the spiritual, and after thoroughly refreshing and rejuvenating the astral body it will find expression in the physical. Hence no real healing of physical ills can be effectual until a correlation is made with the One Life. By correlation is meant free and unimpeded communication with and circulation of spiritual life through all your bodies, so that the will of the Father is done on earth even as it is in heaven.

May 11th, 1908.
"I am now entering a fast which by the intuitions at its finish brings to me or brings me into those Christ powers, to attain which each Neophyte enters the Path."

We would warn you against any process of forcing your psychic development, such as fasting and the like, with the expectation of thus securing so-called "Christ-powers." The only way to really secure The Christ-power is to live The Christ life and let the powers develop themselves in a natural way as the result of duty well done, love and supreme devotion and attention to your daily duties. Any abnormal growth which would apparently result from fasting (except under very exceptional circumstances, which are not present in your case) would be but a mushroom growth, the result of weakness and hysteria, not strength. Especially would this be true if at such a time the duties of your life called for all your physical strength to fulfill them properly, and while your husband and family were making just demands upon your physical powers.

The real Christ-power comes as a conqueror of all experiences. It is a perfect atom given into your keeping; and there must be a sound, strong body. The physical must be conquered and controlled, not killed out; and it must be taught through the power of The Christ and not through fasting. Everything that you crush out and weaken must be taken up again and again until you do your full duty by it. If you develop your mental or psychic or spiritual faculties at the expense of the physical, you must incarnate again, but with a poor weak physical body which will tie you down to earth while the strong mental, psychic or spiritual powers developed prematurely long to be free to follow their higher dictates. This is The Law my child, and in love I must warn you. There is no step too common to take; for each has its lesson or it would not be given you. To neglect one step means to come back later and take it up, perhaps all alone. If you break down or lessen your physical health and thus fail in your full duty to your husband and child, when you return to go over the lesson again you may have not only a weak, miserable body, but you may be deprived of a husband's love and a child's care; for that which we fail to fully appreciate the Great Law removes from us. This is the kindest way, and the only way, to teach us. The Great Law works on, and it matters not whether you fail because you believed the Christ-powers could be gained by fasting or not. Your duty is to walk side by side with your husband in strength and love; to be a help-mate to him on all planes, physical as well as mental and spiritual. You have already found The Christ within, then remember that The Christ follower is faithful in everything, the little daily tasks as well as the great ones.

At all times live and eat abstemiously; but so that the physical body is properly nourished, and give as little thought to it as possible. By this means you will find it much easier to dwell in the higher realms. The animal nature, to be the servant of the Real Self, must be well taken care of; well fed, well groomed and comfortable, but not overfed or indulged. Thus taken care of the animal will do far better work and make far fewer demands than one that is starved or ill-treated. You need the animal for your servant, and you need all its powers in their best possible condition, therefore, treat it as you would any other finely bred animal of which you expected great intelligence and great service.

Those who spend much thought on what they shall NOT eat are dwelling in the stable with the animal just as surely as those who spend great thought upon what they shall eat. The Great Master Jesus said: "Take no thought what ye shall eat, nor wherewithall ye shall be clothed; for your heavenly Father knoweth ye have need of all these things." This means literally to get along with as little thought on these matters as is consistent with keeping the animal in good working condition. Make yourself pleasant to the eye, neat and comfortable, then waste no more time about it or in worrying over it. One who dresses in sack-cloth and ashes and lives on bread and water, often thinks more of that eating and drinking and dressing than a comfortable liver. Such things engender spiritual pride, and of all vices spiritual pride is the worst. It is the most detrimental to the Soul's advance because the hardest to cure.

May 19th, 1908.

"I have been quite ill again, and I should like to know just what is the cause of it. . . . and what to do to avoid these spells in the future."

We will try to give you an understanding of the conditions in your case. You have taken a decided step upward and are feeling the change of vibrations. All life is due to vibrations emanating from the great, pulsating Heart of the Unmanifested. Conceive of the pulsations as coming from the center of a circle and radiating outward to the circumference. Draw seven concentric circles and each one will represent a step inward toward the center; and in each the vibrations will become faster and faster, finer and finer; for naturally they slow down as they get farther and farther away from their source, being slowest on the outer rim—the physical plane. Therefore, a body attuned to the vibrations of the physical plane would be subjected to great strain when indrawn to where the vibrations were more rapid. This is so true that if a sudden jump were possible instant disintegration would result. At every step taken by the Soul there must be a readjustment of the particles of the various bodies until they all harmonize with the vibratory unit of the step. This often results in physical illness and, if not understood, the neophyte is apt to grow discouraged and think he is growing worse rather than better. But when understood it is no more alarming or unreasonable than that an eruptive disease should first have to reach its crisis before a cure could be effected; it is all a part of the cure. You have asked that the Lord of Health shall lay His hands upon you, and you must understand that your request is being literally fulfilled. But all that is evil must be cleansed; all our sins, omissions and misapplications of the Law of Health must first be readjusted ere we can be filled with "Life and Love and Purity." This is the only rationale of healing and is recognized by all regular schools of medicine. We so often forget that there is but one law, "As above, so below." You must recognize and realize that the Divine Healer, represented by the Master Jesus, is present with you and has, at your request, laid His hands (powers) upon you. So be still, and patiently trust and love and believe that every step all the way through is but a step toward the great, pulsating Heart of Love which is Life and Health and Immortality. You can retard or accelerate this readjustment by your attitude of mind exactly as a patient can help or hinder a physician in his physical cure.

Jan. 23rd, 1908.

"I have made little progress in occult studies. In one sense I have made a complete failure; am unable to concentrate; am physically weak; have never had the power of concentration, at least so far back as my remembrance goes. My mind seems to be going to pieces. Sometimes I think that I, as an entity, am being disintegrated. Sometimes I think I have acquired all there is for me in this incarnation—that I must pass on, rest and assimilate what I have already learned. . . . I desire the help you offer if so you CAN help me, for I realize that life is a matter of the growth of the soul."

Your cry for help has reached our ears and we understand your difficulty. While your Soul is learning its various lessons the one GREAT LESSON—the key-note of your present incarnation—is only slowly impressing itself upon your brain consciousness, namely, the necessity for a sound mind in a sound body. You lose hold of the steps gained because, through the weakness of the body, your mind grows morbid and the continuity of the three-fold chain—spirit-mind-body—is broken. Bodily weakness should not be looked upon either as a failure or as a karmic debt, altho in some cases it might be either or both. However, no matter what its immediate cause, it is a lesson. Often it is a needed lesson in patience and sympathy for suffering that locks the Soul in such a body; but more often it is a lesson that only a great Soul is ready to learn. But it is one that all Souls must master before passing on, i.e. to so dominate the body of flesh that has been given them to gain experience through that the Soul-impress may be indelibly fixed in its matter.

The first step in this direction awakens within the physical aura an extreme sensitiveness, even physical weakness. If this is correctly understood and lifted up and correlated with the true Source of Life and Strength, it is a help rather than a hindrance. If it is looked upon as an hindrance, and the door is flung open to all the devils of disease, the last state of that man or woman is worse than the first. The thought to hold, in your case, is that your very physical sensitiveness brings you into closer touch with the Great Souls of Compassions (the

Masters of Wisdom) and makes the physical envelope more ethereal. It thus becomes a blessing rather than a curse.

March 17th, 1908.
"My daughter has been very ill, and lately from overwork I have been confined to my room. . . . "

We sympathize with you in your recent illness and are sorry that the HEALING PRAYER did not reach you in time to be used. While we do not take the position that all illness can be cured by prayer, yet, most of the ills from which humanity suffers are not so much the karmic effects of the past as of inharmony in the present life. In the rush and scramble for existence you get out of harmony with Divine Love and at dis-ease with yourself. Hence a period of forced, and generally painful, readjusting and quiet becomes necessary. In all such cases the HEALING PRAYER, if repeated either mentally or aloud, will at once change the vibrations and bring rest and peace, and ultimately health—ease instead of disease.

April 28th, 1908.
"I have few personal sorrows, but the world's sorrows wear my heart away and injure my health, yet I realize that sorrow is the only purifying fount at which the thirsting soul may drink of eternal life and happiness."

We feel that you need a tonic which will clear up the morbid sensitiveness that is literally sapping your life-force. It is a mistake that is often made, and one that is fostered by the teachings of all the orthodox churches, as well as by many other organizations, that sorrow is the only road to purification; that to be miserable is meritorious, and that only through scourging and suffering can we hope for salvation. The truth is that, when we realize how much sorrow there is in the world, and know of a certainty that THOUGHTS ARE THINGS, and that either joy or sadness has the power to spread over a large area, it becomes our duty to be joyful and happy. In fact the very reason for seeking Wisdom and drawing near to God is that our finite eyes may be opened to some of the glory and love "that would not that any perish, but that all have everlasting life." Indeed, all must and shall be saved; and joy is a most potent factor in this salvation.

As to the world's sorrow, while we must sympathize with it and do all in our power to help, yet Wisdom teaches that ALL are God's children; that they work out their salvation in fear and trembling and sorrow only because they refuse to learn the lesson of salvation in any other way. They suffer BECAUSE THEY CHOOSE TO SUFFER, yet God would not have it so. If the world's sorrow oppresses you, remember that the very best you can do toward lifting that heavy load is to make a center of joy and gladness in your own heart. "Rejoice in the Lord; and again I say unto you rejoice." I wish I could impress this word REJOICE upon your mind so that in turn, by the power of your Will, you could impress it upon the consciousness of every atom of your body, which consciousness in the aggregate is your subconscious mind. If you could register this idea of rejoicing within your subconscious mind you would literally breathe health into your body. Try to realize what health really means. It means doing the will of the Father on earth, in your physical body, as it is done in Heaven in your spiritual body by your Higher Self, who is one with the Father; in which body there is no sickness, nor sorrow, nor death. Take up this thought and meditate upon it while constantly repeating the HEALING PRAYER. Also repeat the Lord's Prayer and at the same time feel that you are creating a circle of life and health and joy that is filled with a bright light which sends its beams far out into the darkness to lead many an one to joy and peace.

> "I have been ill. I went to Christian Science for relief. Three weeks ago I felt that I was well. Today the outward sign of ill-health is as conspicuous as ever. The healer says I am cured of the original trouble. If so why should the manifestation reappear?. . . . Either their teachings in many cases do not agree with this Order or I am unable to see the resemblance. . . . Can you help me to see my way?"

We will try to point out to you where we differ from the Christian Scientists; for, while we know that they have gotten hold of a mighty truth, we also know that, like all experimenters in any field, they have not yet had time to grasp all its workings.

Christian Science is a new and modern cult, and the results of their supposed discovery have not been observed long enough for them to mark the ultimate results. Only those who can watch through the ages and can follow the Soul through many incarnations and note the resulting effect of such experiments through many lives, can fully understand the action of the great Law of Healing.

The way that we advise you to help toward bettering earth conditions such as health, poverty etc., is to hold a strong thought that absolute JUSTICE shall prevail, even though it bring suffering. Hold that the patient shall be spiritually enlightened so that whatever the lesson which the sickness, poverty or other unhappiness is intended to teach will be quickly grasped. Understand, the patient must cure himself. No one can do more than aid in the readjustment. The most that a true healer is permitted to do, aside from the use of physical aids, is to send loving, helpful thoughts of an uplifting character,—never to use his personal magnetism or impress his Will upon the patient's subconscious mind.

Often by pouring his personal magnetism (prana) into the aura of a patient or by sheer force of Will, one may so influence another as to temporarily drive away sickness or trouble, but if the real lesson which the sickness or trouble was meant to teach has not been learned by the patient the moment the Will-power is withdrawn the trouble will return. Or, if the Will-power has been strong enough, the trouble may be driven back from off the physical plane to appear upon some higher plane, perhaps in a different form such as some form of nervous disorder or mental trouble. If the Will-power of the healer is exerted to accomplish this then the healer has interfered with The Law, and he or she will find him or herself drawn into the next wave of inharmony that sweeps over the one they tried to help.

Understand clearly, whatever sicknesses, troubles or trials come to a person are either the result of broken law or are conditions given by the Higher Self of the patient to teach certain necessary lessons and thus gain the experience needed to take the Soul a step onward. To throw the troubles off or to push them back by the life-force (prana) or by the Will-power of another and refuse to learn the lessons intended is only to postpone them. The forces of nature give unquestioning obedience to The Law and The Law is that perfect harmony shall prevail upon all planes. All broken contracts and all disobedience to The Law produce inharmony on all planes at the same time. And the persons bringing into action the particular inharmonious note must THEMSELVES readjust every wave of inharmony that has been produced by their acts before harmony can be restored in their lives.

It is not denial of inharmony that settles the score; but a recognition of it and the correction of its cause. If through Will-power you push it aside and apparently gain either health, wealth or some earthly comfort ere the readjustment is made, the inharmony will gather force by the very pushing back and will sweep over you again and again until it is recognized and adjusted. As the great Master Jesus said: "For verily I say unto you, Till heaven and earth pass, one jot or one tittle shall in no wise pass from the law, till all be fulfilled." This is a benign and beneficent law; for it is only by reaping what we have sown, and eating the fruits thereof, that we can ever learn to plant wheat instead of tares.

Therefore, you can see that for a mental healer to control the forces operating against a patient he must first be fully cognizant of (a) just what the forces are, (b) what old karmic conditions they are working out, (c) what important lesson the Higher Self is trying to teach by means of the action of the forces and (d) whether or not the patient has learned the lesson and benefited by the experience. Thus you can see that to fully and intelligently understand all these factors would require almost super-human wisdom and descretion. And to undertake, as so many do, to control or to interfere with those forces, without any conception of the possibilities in which they may be involved, is as foolish as for a child to play with dynamite. You can do it; but only at a terrible risk.

But never cease to help anyone in distress or cease to use all ordinary means to benefit them for fear of interfering with their Karma; for this you cannot do if you devote your energy to the betterment of their spiritual welfare rather than to their physical desires. It is right to do all in your power at all times to help those in distress, and if you bear in mind these facts failure will not discourage you nor will seeming success unduly elate you; for you will understand that at most you have been but a channel through which the Divine Force should flow.

Understand that it is not that we disapprove of individual Christian Scientists, for there are many beautiful Souls among them who are devoting their lives to serve humanity according to their highest conception of right; but we do realize that the cult is but a one-sided glimpse of Truth, and it is therefore far from complete. We do not object, however, to any path provided you remember the main fact that to be whole you must find out why you are sick, and what lesson it was meant to teach. For the moment you do this in that moment the trouble or sickness will fall from you like a garment cast off.

We ask you to repeat the HEALING PRAYER over and

over again, especially morning and evening, and study the lesson and try to grasp the meaning of Divine Healing. Every time you repeat the Prayer let your mind turn to this Center with a full knowledge that here is a Center from which there radiates Love and the healing Christ-force to all. Each one who puts himself into touch with this force must be helped. It is like the Brazen Serpent lifted up by Moses in the wilderness, all who look or come mentally, with child-like love and faith, will be healed in Soul and body.

"I am suffering from an old wound on my right leg just above the knee joint. Fifteen years ago a surgeon cut a hole through the bone and it does not heal, continually discharges pus. I dread another operation as I am 56 years old, otherwise healthy and do not use tobacco or liquor. Have been advised to try Christian Science. Can you give me any advice?"

We do not advise Christian Science for your leg. Altho the only real help and cure for all ills is what we call Divine Healing as explained in the lesson on THE HEALING PRAYER, i.e. the subordinating of the flesh to the Higher or Divine Self and the harmonizing of all atoms to the key-note of Divinity, still this is an advanced step and there are many intermediate ones before it can be made practical in the case of organic disease. Therefore, when there is a physical, anatomical lesion it should be corrected upon its own plane and re-adjusted by physical means that it may the quicker be in a condition to permit the Divine "Life and Love and Purity" to flow through it unimpeded and thus complete the cure.

We differentiate between cure and mere readjustment. That which has gone awry from purely physical causes must be put into a perfect physical condition ere the Divine Life can fill it and harmonize it with the Divine. It is useless to waste force of Will or expend mental activity in endeavoring to readjust what can quite as well be corrected and put in condition for nature to finish, by physical means, thus leaving the Will to be expended upon the higher planes in bringing about the At-one-ment with the Higher Self which will manifest as perfect health on all planes.

Since you say your wound has been discharging pus for years we would judge that there is some chronic necrotic process at work in the bone and that this has become infected, and where pus is present we can only say, Get it out as quickly as possible. Our best advice to you is for you to go to the best surgeon or to the best hospital you know of and have the necrotic tissue removed, for nature has been unable to slough it out after years of her best endeavors and she needs a little help.

If, as you say, you are otherwise healthy and do not use tobacco or liquor you should not dread an operation; for if you had a bad heart or other vital organs you would not be given a general anesthetic. Then, too, the danger of an anesthetic nowadays is very slight; only about one in 16,000 cases taking them as they come, good and bad condition alike. There is a vast difference in the ground for dread of a surgical operation between the conditions under which operations were done fifteen years ago and today; more than the difference between travel in a stage-coach and in a modern limited express. The danger from surgical operations is largely because patients wait until they are about to die and have given up hope of recovery before having the operation performed, even the surgeon consenting only as a last resort. If taken early there is almost no danger, certainly nothing compared to allowing the condition to continue unrelieved.

> "My husband's health is not good, and I have been having a very anxious time He has just commenced to take a remedy that a psychic healer has prescribed and we hope he will be improved."

As to trusting your husband's health to a psychic healer we would say, and say so emphatically that you cannot misunderstand our words, that, in the case of physical diseases, all psychic treatment must be supplementary to the best physical treatment obtainable from the best physician you know of. If a psychic gives a diagnosis, before acting upon that diagnosis go to the best physician or hospital you can reach and have a thorough physical examination. If the doctor's diagnosis agrees in the main with that of the psychic it may be followed under the doctor's direction. In case the psychic gives more subtle symptoms not discovered by the physician, tell him frankly what you suspect, but without letting him know where you got your suspicion. If he fails to find any evidence of such symptoms after several thorough examinations it is well to disregard them. There is so much room for self-deception in the transmission of psychic information that the only safe course to pursue is to prove it. It should always be verified by the conditions found or else should commend itself to your good judgment and common sense and be judged just as the advice given by any friend who was not a trained physician would be judged.

Above all, never take any kind of drug or medicine except upon the prescription of a physician in whose professional skill and moral qualities you have confidence. Magnetic and other psychic treatments and massage are admirable to supplement the other forms of therapeutics, but we warn you against trusting the case in the hands of anyone but a first class physician.

We recommend the HEALING PRAYER to our pupils not to take the place of proper medical treatment, but to bring about that harmony of mind and body which every physician now recognizes as an essential element in the treatment of disease. We give it to bring our pupils into touch with the vibrations of the One Life which are health; for only when a patient is in harmony with the Well-spring of all Life (the Divine) can even the best medical treatment be more than palliative or push back the manifestation of the disease for the time being or into another channel. Divine Healing should go hand in hand with the best treatment science can offer; for, until humanity has entered the psychic world and can function in the psychic body and use the psychic faculties, it must treat physical ills with physical remedies as a basis. All psychic treatment can be depended upon to do is to harmonize the psychic currents and influence the circulation. Hence diseased conditions arising from mental or psychic states or from temporary and functional disorders of the circulation can be cured by psychic means, and psychic treatment can even be an important factor in the cure of organic disease.

Divine Healing or the coming into harmony with the current of the One Life can and will cure in time, but ere it can bring about a cure it must first, as the HEALING PRAYER expresses it, "drive out the atoms of inharmony and disease." To do this they must first be driven from the mental body, the astral body and then out of the physical body, and during this process there will necessarily be a manifestation of the conditions in the physical body until the well known "healing crisis" is reached and the elimination is ended. Psychic currents can cure psychic diseases and greatly influence physical diseases, but the physical remedies should by no means be overlooked or neglected; for the physical states react upon the psychic quite as much as the psychic do upon the physical. Therefore true healing combines all physical agencies with the psychic and the Divine, for these three are one. Divine Healing applied to physical diseases will work out a cure in time, but it may cause a worse condition before it can cause a better.

Our best advice is that your husband should use the same common sense that he would employ if one of his tools was out of order. He would not wait until it was injured beyond repair or until there was not enough left to be worth repairing, but he would have the first break remedied before it got beyond control. Do the same with the bodily machine.

PART VIII

THE SEX PROBLEM

"Have ye not read, that he which made them at the beginning made them male and female. . . . and they twain shall be one flesh? Wherefore they are no more twain, but one flesh. What therefore God hath joined together, let no man put asunder. . . . All men cannot receive this saying, save they to whom it is given." Matthew XIX, 4-11.

June 15th, 1908.

"The union of two Souls on the highest plane will uplift humanity as little else can. In truth, until we love another absorbingly, how can we know the Love of Loves?. . . . Tell me what you think—is it true that there is for each of us a mate? Or is celibacy the ideal?. . . .

You ask what we think of each Soul having a mate. This doctrine, if it can be called such, has indeed been misconstrued and used as an excuse for all sorts of loose and perverted conduct, yet, like all things that are good, but evil when perverted, it holds a divine germ of spiritual truth. This truth is so sacred, and so easily misunderstood and perverted, that the Masters of Wisdom have ever drawn a veil over it. Only the few who evolve to the point where their own hands can draw aside the veil can hope to understand it. The teachings on this subject are generally given direct from teacher to pupil when the pupil is ready.

The great trouble about celibacy has always been that those who were able to perceive something of the results to be attained are apt to forget or overlook all the intermediate steps. It is like standing on a plain and looking up at a mountain. The snow upon the peak shines out white and clear in the light of the sun and is so beautiful that the gazer feels that it is only a little beyond his grasp, and that all he has to do is to keep his eye upon those shining heights and travel on and on. But in reality those heights kiss the sky; their climatic conditions are different; their air is unfitted for the lungs of the dweller of the plain, and the road up the mountain is beset with dangers and pitfalls. The path that seems to lead straight up to the highest pinnacle may in reality skirt a number of deep crevasses, and to safely reach the heights one must make long detours and pass through many dangerous defiles and be subject to many unknown conditions. The conditions at the top may be absolutely harmful to the aspiring climber unless, by long training and with a competent guide, he learns how to avoid the dark and noisome caverns and safely tread The Path to the heights.

Jan. 26th, 1908.

"I long to transmute all the inner forces, 'The animal-sensual' and all that holds man down to the lower planes, into spiritual energy. . . . All sensual desire upon my wife's part has disappeared, and with me great improvement. I realize all things of that nature must be conquered. . . . "

Your difficulty is known to us and we will try to impart to

you the remedy. The trouble is that your mind and heart have outrun your physical development. You are trying to tear open the bud of personality instead of allowing it to unfold in the sunlight of the god of Love. A most important lesson to remember is that the sex powers are the expression of the Divine Creative Force in matter. It is the same force which created the world and all that is therein. Its misuse and debasement is the cause of all the misery and disease and death. It is the Serpent of Wisdom,[1] the Old Serpent, which, when crawling upon the ground fulfills the curse, "Upon thy belly shalt thou go, and dust shalt thou eat all the days of thy life: and I will put enmity between thee and the woman, and between thy seed and her seed." But this Serpent is not evil in itself, only when allowed to crawl upon the ground. Its other aspect is divine, and when lifted up upon the Tree of Life it will literally fulfill the other prophecy of the Serpent, "In the day ye eat thereof, then your eyes shall be opened, and ye shall be as gods, knowing good and evil." Through the power of the Serpent man has eaten of this Tree of Knowledge; but only from its lower branches. So the "Flaming Sword (the Divine Creative Fire) which turned every way" has barred him from Eden. What he has eaten has given him the power of the gods to know the evil, sinking lower than the beasts, and it is only when he turns and looks at the same Fiery Serpent, and lifts it up upon the cross in the wilderness of life, that he shall once more become whole and find the power of the gods to know the good, even as he has had to know the evil.

Remember that every act which evokes the creative power of the Serpent in the flesh creates after the manner of the thoughts held at the time. From the abuse of this power mankind has peopled the astral with sensual monsters which are ever waiting to incarnate and express themselves through man, and which have the power to create after their kind. It is the thought that determines what you create.

May 10th, 1908.

"My opinion emphatically is that the functions of bodily life, nutritive and reproductive, MUST be held sacred to the purposes for which they are intended."

Your idea of the sacredness of the sex forces is quite right. The sex force is the greatest force that is sent into manifesta-

---

[1] See lesson THE SYMBOL OF THE SERPENT.

tion. In fact, it is THE force of manifestation. It is the Great Creative Force by which everything that is is created. But we go still farther and teach that this force CAN create and DOES create, when directed by the Will-power, just what the desires have formulated. If this were understood there would be fewer temptations to pervert this force during youth. It should be used to carry out mental creations instead of being wasted, to the great detriment of both body and Soul.

If the desire is to create a physical body into which a Soul may come into manifestation, then all the power of the Will should be used to produce just the kind of body wanted. On the other hand, should the desire be to re-create your own physical, astral or mental bodies the same force is used, for it creates after the pattern formed by the desires. And, alas! it is this same force which, under the direction of lascivious thoughts and impure and vile imagination, has been expended in creating the entities that prey upon man in the form of sickness, deformity, disease and death. Then, too, when this force is denied a normal physical embodiment it must create upon the mental and astral planes, and there it has created monsters of unspeakable horror (corresponding to, or rather being the embodiment of man's lust) which must, of necessity, attach themselves to their creator and look to him for their redemption: true Frankenstein monsters that cannot be mastered except through a strong, determined effort to create their opposites and to withold the life-force from them.

As you must clearly understand, since every expenditure of this force, for whatever purpose, creates something some where, can you wonder at the misery of the world? Or can you fail to see where the entering wedge must be placed for the redemption of the world? In reality this is the work which this Movement was established to perform, namely, to go down into the mire of the sex question and rescue the precious pearls that have been cast before the swine, i.e. to teach the right use of the sex function throughout all creation. The mineral, the vegetable, the animal each have the power, through the use of the creative force of the One Life, to create after their kind; but man has an added power—and the consequent added responsibility—to create not merely after his kind—to which creation the lower kingdoms are limited but, through the power of his Will, to create anything he desires. Thus far the will has been to create for himself, and for the Race, only evil or devils; for "By man came death into the world and by man must also come the resurrection from the dead." He has eaten of the Tree of Knowledge and has become "as the gods" to know the evil and now he must become "as the gods" to know the good. These are the truths concerning the sex functions for which this Order stands.

March 4th, 1908.

"Why is it that we find such a dearth of children in the so-called 'well bred people' or good class families? About 40% perhaps are without children, the rest with one or two. The ordinary answer is, of course, that it is due to the use of preventives, etc. . . . In the vegetable world, where my real question lies, some types and forms are already in trouble giving but few seeds, the sweet pea for instance. The largest and best in every way gives but few seeds. . . . Is it because ordinary methods of crossing are like human intermarriage between relatives?"

The reason that fewer monads are incarnating in the so-called cultured class is chiefly because the culture of the world is in no way an advantage to the perfection of vigor of the body, nor its environments such as to materially help the Soul onward in its appointed task. The Soul chooses its own environments in accordance with the conditions best suited to help it along in its chosen path. Physical obstacles such as poverty, the necessity for mingling with humanity en masse and in the pushing and crowding generally found in the so-called lower ranks of society, are not only great helps to the attainment of perfection if conquered, but if the incarnating Soul is at all advanced and has a realizing sense of the great love of Brotherhood, its most overwhelming desire is to incarnate where it can help on in the work of the redemption of the Race. This can be done more effectively by one who has mingled with the lower strata and has felt its deep heart-throbs of misery, and even of crime. Such an one grows nearer to his brother man, and by his very struggle to get above the conditions is capable of a deeper realization, through his own suffering, of the suffering of humanity and gains more sympathy with its needs.

Those born into affluence have no such chance. The temptations of idleness and the deadening effects of selfishness are harder to conquer, hence only such Souls as have either not advanced to the point of at-one-ment with humanity and desire only personal ease, or advanced Souls who know the danger yet, having conquered the temptations of the lower levels in former lives, deliberately choose such an incarnation that they may have the means to help humanity on a larger scale. Necessarily these are few; one here and there.

As to the same thing taking place in plant life, the cause is more apt to be that, this being an experimental age in that line, man has not yet learned how to increase vigor in the plant. That is to say, a plant has only a certain amount of life-force and this, man, by his Will, has directed we will say into the line of a perfect blossom; but at the expense of the power of propagation. The lesson to learn is how to draw more life into the plant and balance it so that there will be enough for both activities.

March 3rd, 1908.

"Can you explain why my wife and I seem to be gradually growing apart? There is no quarrel between us at all, only distress that we cannot have more than a friendly, chummy relation. . . . "

As to the general proposition, the mere fact that a man and woman do not belong together is all-sufficient. The Law back of this is the fact that the general plan of all humanity was laid down at the beginning of this manvantara according to strict geometrical lines. Since the time of the separation of the sexes (at the end of the Third Root-Race) these lines have been mixed up more and more, until now they are in the greatest confusion. But the time has come when the straightening out process has begun in earnest. The real meaning of redemption is that The Christ (the living force of the Divine Creative Fire—the Law of God) must redeem from this intricate confusion all the various geometrical lines (Souls) and put each in its proper place again in the grand plan. Sin is inharmony, the separation of the positive and negative parts of a line, or a snarling of the strands like that seen in a tangled skein of yarn. Redemption means redeeming, a bringing back to the original condition; for you cannot redeem a thing that you have not once had and lost. Therefore the very first step toward growth is to work toward the straightening out of the tangled lines. But in accomplishing this you must place yourself unresentfully in the hands of the Lords of Karma, which means holding the attitude of "Thy will be done." When this is done you at once find that in exact accord with your sincerity The Law will begin to work out. At first it will precipitate upon you all your old Karma. That must be accepted and worked out cheerfully.

March 3rd, 1908.

"You must decide for me if I am ready for the probationer's course, and if my husband is ready also; for I will not begin till he, too, is ready. We have come thus far together and I will wait many years if need be until he is ready."

Your attitude of desiring to go hand in hand with your husband is the right one; for no other way is possible. When two persons are really joined in a true marriage of the Soul, as in your case, it is impossible for one to advance without the other. Sometimes the forward impulse seems to come from one and sometimes from the other, but in reality all true spiritual growth is flowing to them jointly. They have reached a point where, from the soul plane or plane of causes, from which the Masters see them and on which they come into contact with the Great White Lodge, THEY ARE REALLY ONE, and all spiritual impulses are given to them AS ONE. This is the universal but sadly neglected meaning of the words of the marriage ceremony "Whom God hath joined let no man put asunder." Alas, it is but a very few couples whom God hath joined. When man only hath joined them it is only the bodies that are joined, not the Souls. In such cases all real spiritual advance must necessarily push them asunder, because their Souls, not being one, cannot follow the same upward Path; each must ultimately find its own.

"In an occult pamphlet I note the statement that for the birth of an advanced Soul, an Avatar for instance, it is not essential that he be born of what the world calls a sexually pure woman. Is this correct?" Inquirer, Spokane, Wash.

Most emphatically no. The conception of such a Divine Emanation in human form can only take place between specially prepared and absolutely pure parents. Moreover, they must be perfectly affinitized or harmonized upon all planes, physical, mental and spiritual. They must be set apart and sanctified long ere such a conception could be a possibility. They must be lawfully wedded in the sight of men, according to the laws of the land, and must be blameless in the sight of God and man. This, however, does not mean that they must never have sinned in the past; but it does mean that long before such a conception could take place they must have washed their garments (bodies) pure and white in the blood[1] of the Lamb, i.e. the spiritual life-force poured out for humanity by the sacrificial Lamb or The Christ power—the Word made flesh and sacrificed that humanity might be redeemed. Through this force such parents must have gained purity of body, purity of mind and purity of heart, the attainment of which will necessarily express itself in purity of life. Any exception to this is unthinkable.

(Published in THE HOUSE OF THE INTERPRETER)

"Wrote you a day or so ago, a large portion of my letter being devoted to the sex question; and yesterday had a discussion with. . . . trying to find out what the position of the Fifteen is on that subject. . . . It is rather curious that. . . . are morbidly inclined to regard the union of the sexes as improper under all conditions—even within marriage—except for the sake of procreation. . . . They then brought up the charges against. . . . as published in the. . . . , and his admission of the facts charged. I quite agreed with them in their objection to. . . . I think that was the substance of that line of discussion."

We would warn you that it is not well to allow your mind to dwell upon the sex problem or to talk of it unnecessarily, not because it is evil to do so, but because it is one of the most sacred of mysteries, and is not to be handled with unclean or profane hands. Like many other precious things, it changes its whole aspect when ruthlessly dragged forth for inspection. Then it becomes dead and putrified. It should be guarded most sacredly. Remember that which everyone condemns generally has some inherent reason in it for such condemnation, and this question as a topic for conversation is no exception. You cannot allow your mortal mind to dwell upon it for any length of time without arousing lust, and to make it the subject of social conversation awakens lustful thoughts in others. Therefore we ask you, as a member of the Order, to use all your influence toward avoiding any such discussions and to communicate this request to others of the Order with whom you come in touch.

It is neither necessary nor advisable to analyze this force. Just hold to the idea of PURITY. Think how to be pure in mind and body, and leave the rest. But, once for all, if it will help you to turn your mind away from this subject, we will say

---

[1] See lesson on A BRIEF OUTLINE OF EVOLUTION.

that we approve of sex relations ONLY between those who are united in true spiritual love, and in the LEGITIMATE, LEGAL MARRIAGE relation. It should be used for purposes of creation, but the creation need not be a physical body; for they can consciously create an immortal body for themselves, or can create any other great work. If one should be so situated that he finds the one to whom he feels he belongs outside the legitimate marriage relation, let him understand that this is the result of Karma and shows that for some reason they have been separated to learn certain lessons independently. Any attempt to break through or over-leap the barriers that separate them would but build up fresh karmic suffering. Understand this point clearly, THEY CANNOT BELONG TO EACH OTHER SEXUALLY UNTIL THE BARRIERS HAVE BEEN REMOVED so that they can be UNITED BY THE LAWS OF THE LAND and stand before the world in perfect purity. THERE IS NO EXCEPTION. Those who belong together will always be together on the higher planes, and between incarnations; but if separated upon the earth plane they must patiently learn their lessons and work out the Karma that holds them apart. If they do not do so it entails another life under similar conditions. They will be sure to incarnate together when each is ready to learn the lessons which they can only learn together.

If your spiritual Will is not strong enough to create the qualities you need in your character, then create upon the mental plane. When you feel the force moving within you say, "I must create, what shall it be?" Then look around you and see what new thing you can turn your attention to. If you can write, start some little article, and if it is not worth publishing at least you can make a start and go over and over it improving it each time. Take up some new task or duty. Do some kind, unselfish act that will require some time and thought and effort to accomplish. In this way you will divert the current of the Divine Creative Force into a normal channel of expression. SO-CALLED "PHYSICAL RELIEF" IS NEVER NECESSARY, and to teach that it is permissible is but to cloak animal desire in words that make it seem respectable.

Do not say that you cannot thus divert your creative force into accomplishments for good, for it has been successfully done by hundreds of pupils, and has brought peace and joy and happiness and purity of mind and spiritual advancement to all who have learned it. The teachings of this Order are not for some superhuman life, but for the average, decent, clean-minded person on the physical plane. They are not vague theories, but practical instructions for daily life. They are not impossible speculations as to what we can do in some future manvantara, but plain statements of what hundreds have proved and are showing forth in their lives RIGHT HERE AND NOW. Further more, we teach that under no circumstances can an evil or impure thing upon the earth plane ever become anything but evil and impure on the higher planes; for all planes are one, and what is impure on one is impure on all. UNDER NO CIRCUMSTANCES CAN EVIL OR IMPURE ACTS ON THE PHYSICAL PLANE CAUSE SPIRITUAL GROWTH; for the acts themselves are creating exactly the opposite conditions. Those who are teaching such abominable doctrines under the name of Esoteric Theosophy, or under the guise of obtaining some sort of spiritual development, will have a terrible Karma to answer for in the future. We cannot emphasize too strongly the fact that there can be no spiritual teachings, either esoteric or exoteric, that are not spotless in their purity ON ALL PLANES; for The Christ can dwell only with the pure in heart.

We not only denounce such vile doctrines, but we are trying to lead humanity back into paths of natural purity. Hence, as our lesson on CELIBACY plainly states, we believe that all teachings that prohibit true and legal marriage under any pretext, and which foster unnatural suppression of the life forces ere humanity, even in a small decree, has learned the lessons of pure love and the possibility of real spiritual marriage, any such teachings, we repeat, are a menace to society and but cause abnormal expression of the forces thus repressed. As we say in PURITY: "When confined to the physical plane man is apt to lose control of it" etc., and all forms of abnormality and all efforts to separate this force from the spiritual plane is confining it to the animal. And if we give it over to the animal and then deny that animal a normal way of expressing it, just so sure will some vile and abnormal way of gratification be imagined. This alone should be proof to a thinking mind that such teachings are abnormal. Our students must learn that this force does not belong to the animal plane alone. And they must grasp the higher and deeper truth that marriage does not belong merely to the animal plane, but has its correspondence on all planes. Hence the great and crying need of love and purity in the marriage relation.

While we know that the sinner is in reality but an outward expression of the combined thought of the whole community, and that not one is without sin or capable of casting the first stone, still it is our duty to set our faces, in no uncertain manner, against all such crimes against the Holy Temple of the Living Christ as those to which you refer. This is the attitude of THE ORDER OF THE 15. We have come into manifestation as a protest against the befouling of all mankind and of everything sacred with the slime of the serpent; and above all in the name of Theosophy! and for "spiritual advancement"! We must and shall use all our influence unceasingly against such teachings and proclaim PURITY. But we also go deeper and show some of the causes that have produced this abomination that is paraded boldly before the children of men, being defended even by the chosen ones of the. . . . Society in their official publications!

The teaching that all sex relations are inherently impure and evil, and that they should be killed out and marriage discouraged and discountenanced, IS A WRONG AND PERNICIOUS DOCTRINE. And as long as such teachings find credence, human nature, like a flowing river which is dammed up, will find an outlet in some abnormal manner. And if the barriers of false teachings are not speedily removed and the true and normal channel purified and cleared from obstructions, it will inundate the entire Race.

> "I note that you emphasize 'legal marriage' as the sole condition of intimate relationship between lovers. This seems to me an arbitrary dictum. Social and economic conditions are such that many legally married couples who do not love each other in purity, who in fact repel each other, cannot separate without pain and distress to those dependent upon them and to whom they owe conformity to public standards. Should one in this legal situation refuse to express love through that divine and ineffable relation, even though that love is pure? In other words: Does the legal contract entered into during years of ignorance bar one from what would otherwise be a sacred, beautiful, vital love?"

Legal marriage by no means insures purity; but even if it fails in this respect that failure does not mean that marriage was not intended to fulfill the Law of Opposites in perfect purity. Impurity arises because the contracting parties have broken The Law, and the Master Jesus said: "Till heaven and earth pass, one jot or one tittle shall in no wise pass from the law, until all be fulfilled." While there is but one Great Law governing the universe, yet it has seven manifestations, and the words "jot and tittle," altho now obsolete, were used to indicate these seven manifestations.

The Great Law first manifests as (a) Order. This means that everything is tending toward perfection in its proper place. The only reason why one particular jot or tittle is not fulfilled is that there are six other related jots or tittles which must also be fulfilled.

The second manifestation is as (b) Compensation. In every event there is a compensation. You can learn it by comparison, "As above, so below."

The Great Law works as (c) Cause and Effect or Karma. "Whatsoever a man soweth, that shall he also reap."

The Law also expresses as (d) Vibration, (e) as Balance, in (f) Cycles and (g) as Polarity. It thus begins with Orderly Sequence and ends or is completed by Polarity. Karma is by no means all The Law; it is but one of its phases.

The above, when applied to the marriage relation, means that only true marriage—that which is made in Heaven—can fulfill The Law in all its manifestations. If the union does not fulfill the laws of man it is not fulfilling The Law as Order. If it is not a marriage of love and purity then it is not fulfilling The Law as Vibration and as Polarity (opposites). It may, however, be fulfilling other manifestations of The Law. An unhappy marriage may be fulfilling The Law as Karma. That is, it may be the result of causes set up and not worked out in a past life. This result must be worked out through fulfillment ere The Law can work in its fulness in the other manifestations and bring you to your true polar center to be one with your true complement, who alone can fulfill The Law with you.

Such an unhappy marriage, be it ever so irksome, must be in accord with some manifestation of The Law, and hence is not to be set aside or terminated except through fulfillment. Were it not in accord with The Law there would be nothing to hold you to it and it would pass out of your life and release you with scarcely a ripple. If no other manifestation can be found The Law works as Compensation, i.e. the situation will bring you something to be gained either as experience, as duty to perform or as the joy of Parenthood etc. Indeed, many marriages are brought about and consummated by The Law working as Compensation alone.

From the above you will see that marriage, even if only an earthly bond, is, nevertheless, a part of The Law and is not to be set aside until "all be fulfilled." If another love obtrudes itself upon you, which it is pretty sure to do if you are not married to your true polar opposite, the marriage becomes your GREAT TEST. Your new love may be pure, in fact IF IT IS LOVE IT WILL BE PURE, but you have no right to it until you have fulfilled the manifestation of The Law under which you find yourself. And it cannot be consummated upon the physical plane without breaking The Law and defiling its purity. To seize it before you have fulfilled the old bond necessitates another long experience of separateness until the old bond is fulfilled and the two can become one on earth in perfect purity, even as they are one in heaven.

If you believed in only one life-period your attitude would, perhaps, be reasonable; but you know that each earth life is but one day at school, and that you can never graduate until you have completed and mastered the course of training laid down. Understanding this, however, you grow patient; for, like the boy at school, if you play truant and run away to go fishing with the girl of your heart, you know that the few stolen hours of joy in her company have robbed you of the opportunity of enjoying her society in much greater completeness after school is over.

Know, absolutely, that The Law IS and that it MUST work out. If one jot or tittle of The Law could go wrong in your personal affairs, all creation would be thrown out of harmony. Hence, sooner or later, you must fulfill The Law in love. And to repudiate any present duty or obligation to apparently hasten that fulfillment is but to stay the longer after school and put the time of fulfillment farther away. You cannot fulfill The Law unless you are pure, and you cannot be pure while you violate any manifestation of The Law.

If you are only held by the law of man you must fulfill that law in purity and learn its lessons until the end. If you have made the vow to "love her, comfort her, honor, and keep her in sickness and in health; and, forsaking all others, keep thee only unto her, so long as ye both shall live," rest assured that The Law will require that vow of you unto the last jot and tittle. But that vow once fulfilled, you will not be bound in a future day at school.

However, if all parties to the vow agree to dissolve it, and if there are no circumstances or duties that prevent its dissolution, the vow no longer holds, or rather it has been fulfilled. But as long as one of the parties to the vow, either the man, the woman or the law of man, holds to it the vow is binding until fulfilled. Understand this point clearly, only by the consent of All the parties, the man, the woman and the law of the land, can the vow be fulfilled and the bond dissolved. But in the event of either party wilfully breaking the vow, and if because of this the injured party is willing to waive his or her claims to the fulfillment of the vow, then he or she is free in the eyes of the law of God; for a vow that is broken is annulled, and the law of the land will grant the injured one legal freedom.

July 11th, 1908.

"I must tell you frankly that I cannot agree with some of your teachings. . . . The celibacy, for instance, of the Brahmins in the east and those desiring spiritual development, after fulfilling all the requirements of the marriage states, by mutual consent, in a spiritual sense, as Jesus said making themselves eunuchs for the kingdom of heaven's sake. He that is able to receive it, let him receive it'. . . . Jesus, John, Paul, the Adepts, the Masters and Mystics of all ages have neither married nor advocated it."

You make very sweeping statements as to Jesus, John, Paul, the Adepts, etc., for which you have no authentic data. In fact, if you were able to read between the lines and within the letter of all authentic teachings handed down from the Great Teachers, you would soon change your mind. In seeking for these truths is it necessary to take the teachings of the Great Ones direct as they fall from Their lips, or as little adulterated by human explanations as it is possible to obtain them. The ones you mention may or may not have married on the physical plane. History cannot always be relied upon in such cases, as it is generally made to conform to the ideas of the followers several hundred years afterward as to what the Teacher should have done.

As society is now constituted and with so many crass failures and quarrels and vile slanders among so-called leaders, all of which are so many stumbling-blocks in the way of God's children, it is most necessary that all things are done so that even the children of this world may have no excuse for mis-

The Sex Problem

understanding, and so that no moral law be violated, but that "Ye shall render unto Caesar the things that be Caesar's and unto God the things that be God's." The time has come, and this is primarily the Movement, for uplifting the masses and preparing the whole race to take a higher step in evolution. The Lodge of Masters, who always work with the cosmic currents, understand this. This is not a period of individual advance or of the helping of all by picking out the few and leading them on to perfection. That was a necessary way to work in other periods of the world's history and that was the way chosen, the reason being that when the period now at hand should come there would be those who would be ready to take up the work for the masses. Now all work is along entirely different lines. The disciples chosen to prepare for the coming Avatar must be able and willing to give up self, even selfadvancement, and live among men exemplifying in all things purity, honesty and all the virtues approved of by the world, that the world may see and understand. They must be careful to make no wide separation, no gulf, over which the flocks (the sheep) cannot easily leap; for the whole flock must be led into green pastures and beside still waters.

If you teach the masses that to gain Heaven they must give up normal living and become celibates, the result must inevitably be, as it has always proved in the past, absolutely abortive in so far as the masses are concerned. Cast your eye backward over history and honestly ask yourself if celibacy has proved an effective way of saving or helping the world? Has it not rather made a wide gulf or separation? the monks and celibates on the one hand, swollen with spiritual pride, "I am holier than thou" written all over them, or at the best, hidden in caves, forgotten of mankind, their very lives unlived through austerity, making very little impression upon the community in which they lived. On the other hand the masses, God's little ones, the sheep of His fold, hopelessly wallowing in the mire of sensuality, a prey to the wolves of desire and passion, relegating, in a sort of hopeless despair, all personal salvation and religious observances to those who, in the eyes of the masses, are set apart to attend to it.

Under all the seeming perversity and evil of humanity there runs a strong current of common-sense and justice. A close student of sociology must admit that underlying all the rules of conventionality and so-called worldly wisdom, in fact the root from which these have sprung, there exists some vital truth that cannot safely be ignored. The world knows that the instincts implanted in the human heart are of God and are necessary for the development and advancement of the race; that the married state is holy and that it embraces and brings forth and makes possible all that is most uplifting and sacred in human life. Therefore, when taught that the normal functioning of these natural instincts are of the Devil, their sense of justice is outraged and they choose the Devil for a master. Since they are taught that there is no hope of reaching perfection in a natural way, they turn their backs upon an unjust God, leaving that conception of God to those who, either from spiritual pride or because all normal instincts are burned out owing to abuse in past lives, or who have never cultivated the heart center, are self-elected to stand as the advocates of those whom THEY consider lost sheep.

This whole plan must now be changed. The first ones to walk the new path must expect stones, mud and gibes from those of the old regimen. Many will say of them, as was said of the Master Jesus, that they consort with sinners and eat bread (symbolic of spiritual food) with them. In fact, this taunt alone, if rightly taken and understood in its real meaning, would be a positive refutation of the assertion you make about Jesus. But there are many more refutations. We will take the chapter from which you quote, remembering always that the Bible, instead of being a history of necessarily physical events, is a gathering together of parables and teachings. Taking this view one of the greatest objections to it is removed, namely that the events following consecutively have no bearing on each other; for it has been proved that they occurred at widely separated times and places. They follow each other consecutively because that order is necessary to bear out the lesson being taught. In other words, a series of narratives is related which may or may not have happened; but it does not matter, as they are merely tales to illustrate the point at issue. They are placed together because they emphasize differing phases of the one lesson. Let us take the chapter from which you quote.

First it is recorded that: "The Pharisees came unto him, tempting him, and saying unto him, Is it lawful for a man to put away his wife for every cause? And he answered and said unto them, Have ye not read, that he which made them at the beginning made them male and female. . . . Wherefore they are no more twain, but one flesh. What therefore God hath joined together, let not man put asunder." The Pharisees then went on to ask about divorce. Jesus answered: "Moses because of the hardness of your hearts suffered you to put away your wives: but from the beginning it was not so." This plainly means that it is possible, because of dense physical vibrations of passion alone, to be joined by man with no spiritual marriage by God. In such a case it is not only lawful, but necessary for the advancement of each for them to separate. Then His disciples, who evidently were imbued with the same teachings that are now puzzling you, said, "If the case of the man be so with his wife, it is not good to marry." But the significant answer of Jesus plainly shows that He was not, as generally interpreted, apologizing for saying so positively that God did join twain into one flesh, for this would put Him in a most vacillating position. His answer was to show why there were instances when the exception proved the rule. This is so plain that it is remarkable that people of common-sense can so twist it as to make it apparently mean exactly the opposite, following as it does the reasons for separation and being a direct answer to the statement, "It is not good to marry." "All men cannot receive this saying, save they to whom it is given." "This saying" was manifestly "Wherefore they are no more twain, but one flesh. What therefore God hath joined together, let no man put asunder." Then He goes on to say what you quote above about eunuchs. This, if read as a continuation of the same remark, shows plainly that Jesus did not mean to commend or approve of eunuchs—for in another place the making of eunuchs is expressly forbidden—but meant to show why man could not understand "this saying." It was in substance the same teaching that I am now giving you.

Immediately a new parable is introduced, namely, "Suffer little children, and forbid them not, to come unto me." This is a strong confirmation that those who will enter the Kingdom are not those who have made eunuchs of themselves for the kingdom of heaven's sake (a eunuch being a mutilation of the divine form, an abnormal and imperfect man), but those who have become as little children. This is then followed by the story of the rich young man, rich in psychic gifts, an earnest follower of YOGI practices etc. "All these things have I kept from my youth up," i.e. the commandments, the austerities and practices and observances of the law. But Jesus told him, "Sell that thou hast and give to the poor, and thou shalt have treasure in heaven: and come and follow me," i.e. The Christ. After this follows the so much misunderstood saying, "It is easier for a camel to go through the eye of a needle, than for a rich man to enter into the kingdom of God." This means that there is a wider separation between a mere animal's developing its psychic faculties—for only by functioning in the fourth dimension could a camel pass through the eye of a needle—than for a man rich in psychic development, who at the same time set himself apart from others and was puffed up with spiritual pride and in danger of resting on his own superior knowledge, to enter the kingdom of heaven. The last paragraph of that chapter positively confirms the idea that all these parables were dealing with one and the same lesson. "But many that are first shall be last; and the last shall be first."

Another passage so frequently quoted in this connection is, "But they which shall be accounted worthy to obtain that world, and the resurrection from the dead, neither marry, nor are given in marriage; neither can they die any more. . . . being the children of the resurrection." The explanation is that spiritual marriage once made can never be unmade—the one flesh can never again become twain. Naturally those who attain the resurrection will neither marry nor be given in marriage because they are married for all eternity; they have learned their earthly lesson. We might as well say that it is wrong to die because perfected Souls will die no more. "Whoso hath ears to hear and heart to comprehend, let him hear."

May 23rd, 1908.

"What is your advice to one who is troubled with impure thoughts and dreams on the sex question?"

Recognize that the sex force is the Great Creative Force; that it is given to man as his crowning glory. It is also man's greatest test, the test being not that he must kill it out, as so many teach, but that he use it aright. As soon as you recognize this grand truth you at once ask, What am I expected to create? You know that it can only occasionally be used to create a tabernacle in which an immortal Soul can dwell, and this of course only in the legitimate marriage relation. And even on these occasions it must be taken up seriously, earnestly, in perfect purity and with spiritual aspirations, and then only under the most favorable circumstances. But, you ask, what about its use at all other times? Bear in mind that procreation is not the only use of this power; for when guided by the Will it creates whatever man desires. In the lower animals it is but a function for perpetuating the species, hence its call ceases to be persistent when the proper season is past, unless, through association with mankind, the animal has become abnormal in this respect; but with man there are no seasons, there are no seasons or times when it is more persistent than at others. This shows that man is expected to use his faculty of creative thought to harness this great river of creative force and make it create for him according to his Will.

Our advice then is to give this matter no more attention than any other normal function receives. That is, see that it is put to its proper use; see that it does not become your master and take up an undue amount of your thought, but that it is kept an obedient servant ready to do your will when called upon. If you feel its call persistently, or if you find yourself growing irritable with no apparent reason, say to yourself, "I am a creator, what shall I create?" Then turn your mind at once to something you desire to accomplish, knowing that this force is the power that will create for you the objects of your desires. It will create within you such desirable qualities as you find you lack. If you have a fault you wish to correct, create its opposite. Think no more about the fault, but put all your thought on its opposite. For instance, if you are given to evil imaginings on this subject, when you feel the creative power coming upon you at once begin to create lofty ideals and thoughts of purity. Understand that nothing can come to you that you yourself do not admit within your aura. The impure thought-forms are your own creations, created by the impure use of the creative force. Strive, then, with all your might to send out thought-forms of purity in such numbers and with such power that they will transmute and redeem the impure ones.

Remember that thoughts are things and must express through their creator. Man is under absolute bondage to thought. Thought-forms surround him and draw their life from him. If evil, they tempt him to pour out fresh force in evil channels that they may gain more life; for thoughts similar to themselves supply them with energy, while thoughts of purity withhold life from them. The VOICE OF THE SILENCE says, "If thou wouldst not be slain by them, then must thou harmless make thy own creations, the children of thy thoughts, unseen, impalpable, that swarm round humankind, the progeny and heirs to man and his terrestrial spoils." Create thoughts of purity, chastity, control, etc. and divert the physical force by at once beginning some definite line of work; if not in building up your character, then in some kind of mental work, realizing that you are consciously using your creative force. Sit down and write an article embodying just what you desire to create within yourself or your idea of what perfect purity means. If this is not convenient, begin some task with your hands, something that will involve manual labor and require thought and energy for its execution. Do some kind unselfish act for another that will necessitate thought and careful planning not to wound; something that would remain undone but for your efforts. Take a tramp out in the open to some objective point, observing the harmony and beauty of nature, and realize how everything in nature has its normal place and its normal and natural use until perverted by man. Realize that you are asserting your prerogative as a creator and that the sex force is the motive power which you are using. If you do any of these things you will not have to puzzle yourself about how the force is transmuted into mental energy or with finding out the particular path by which it reaches the brain, and yet you will divert its expression from the physical organs to the mental plane in a perfectly normal way. If you furnish the thought-forms and the Will to create purity, the forces will follow out your directions without your having to go into particulars. Above all, you will divert your attention from the physical expression of this force.

If you should have a failure in following this plan, waste no thought upon it, but pick yourself up and with more determination than ever strive to create around you thought-forms of purity, and of helpfulness to others; for these must express through you and will strengthen you for the future.

Each night before retiring repeat the HEALING PRAYER and say repeatedly, until you have impressed it upon your subconscious mind, "I refuse to create! I refuse to create this night!" Then when impure dreams come to you you will be able to conquer even before you awake and realize what has happened. Put your failures behind you. Give them no more force by thinking of them or worrying about them. Live each day and each night for itself; for if you can conquer one day at a time you conquer all.

Hundreds of students have followed this plan and have found it practical. You can do the same. But do not expect to master the question in a day. This force is like any other, it sweeps you off your feet only when you place yourself under it. Harness it by your Will-power and you are its master and it a most wonderful servant.

PART IX

SPIRITUAL GROWTH AND DEVELOPMENT

"Now we have received, not the spirit of the world, but the spirit which is of God; that we might know the things that are freely given to us of God. Which things we also speak, not in the words which man's wisdom teacheth, but which the Holy Ghost teacheth; comparing spiritual things with spiritual. But the natural man receiveth not the things of the Spirit of God: for they are foolishness unto him: neither can he know them, because they are spiritually discerned." I Corinthians, II, 12-14.

"Men who are devoid of the power of spiritual perception are unable to recognize the existence of anything that cannot be seen externally." Paracelsus.

July 6th, 1908.
"For a period of several weeks I was able to know how to help my fellows in many ways, not of my own power but by a wonderful love of the Creator. Much of this capacity has now left me, owing I believe to my spiritual pride, but this world is now a different place. This exaltation of spirit was looked upon by those nearest and dearest as a sign of brain trouble, but if it is I am happier with it than without. . . . Now I want help to develop the powers I possess, as I hope it may be given to me to help others. If your teachings are such as will show me how to grow without appearing abnormal in my actions. . . . I will thankfully and patiently learn. . . . But duties to those nearest and dearest hold me back."

The experience of which you speak was a momentary opening of the Third Eye—the pineal gland. This sometimes happens before the disciple has learned to function consciously on the soul plane and is a foretaste of what you can look forward to in the future. As you say, spiritual pride would quickly cause you to fall backward on The Path. If you are conscious of the temptation and are making earnest efforts to conquer and are sincerely working from the standpoint of love for your fellow men, the mere fact of the discontinuance of the soul-faculty of reaching up into the higher realms and drawing direct from the Fount of all Wisdom should not discourage you. The Third Eye sometimes opens in moments of great spiritual exaltation or in deep meditation, and then closes again; but if you retained the faculty of knowing for some weeks, it is surely the result of conscious effort and is an index of soul development, either in this or past lives.

Since all phenomena, either familiar or the so-called supernatural, is subject to the law of "the pairs of opposites," it follows the rhythmic Law of Activity and Passivity, out-breathing and in-breathing, day and night. After a period of manifestation there would naturally follow a period of indrawing, a night period. Instead of this being a loss it is just as necessary as is the night. It is a period in which to rest and recuperate your faculties. It is only in these periods of indrawing and rest that, if we understand the Law and make a mental effort through study and meditation, we can digest what has been given to us, so that when the day-period again dawns we will be ready to use the power wisely, understandingly and under full control of the Will. Do not waste time lamenting the fact that the night has come, but use the time to renew your strength so that when the morning dawns you will be able to go forth in the power and might of the Living Christ to uplift the fallen, comfort the feeble and the weak and work for the good of all.

A word of caution, Brother, when the exaltation cometh. Try to hold it subject to the Will. Be not unduly elated; for "He that ruleth himself is greater than he who taketh a city." It takes a stronger man to rule himself when under the powerful exaltation of Divine Wisdom than it does to rule the lower appetites. Just as far as the pendulum swings to one side must it swing back again. If we exhaust ourselves in one day, the night must be long and spent in sleep; but if we conquer Self and remain calm and dispassionate, the days and nights will be equal, or even with only a short period of rest between, so that one may work steadily on without being depressed during each night-period.

To develop your powers study Nature. Grow as the flower grows. You love the sun (The Christ) because through it you must unfold whatever is good within you and give it out for the good of mankind. Pay no more attention to the manner of your unfolding than does the rose. Open your heart to The Christ and grow. Jesus said, "If ye have faith as a grain of mustard seed, ye shall say unto this mountain, Remove hence to yonder place; and it shall remove; and nothing shall be impossible unto you." That is the kind of faith you must have—faith that within you is the germ of The Christ power, and that through it you can fulfill all the law of your being. The tiny grain of mustard seed never doubts but that it has the power to grow into a tree in which the birds of the air shall lodge, apparently impossible though this may seem while a seed. It obeys the law of its being and just grows on in perfect faith that it has the power to fulfill its destiny. If you bask in the Sun of Righteousness, to keep from growing normally would be impossible. Learn to love, and forget. Become so interested in works of mercy and helpfulness that you will know that you are growing only by the perfume of good that surrounds you, and by your increased ability to help others.

Leave no duty, no matter how humble, undone. The nearest and dearest would not be the nearest and dearest if your first duty were not to them. The mustard tree and the rose take to themselves and assimilate only the pollen of their kind, and must do so ere they can bring forth and grow to perfection. But this does not deter them from spreading their branches to the sun and making a nesting place for the birds and giving out nectar (which when transmuted into honey by the bees, becomes food for man); shelter for cattle and grateful shade and comfort for all created things. All this by just growing naturally in their place. Take the little duties as they come, for not one step can be missed. The man who is always looking at the top of the mountain stumbles over the jagged rocks at its base; but the man who is so busy helping others to climb that he has no time to stand gazing at the heights is the one who gets to the top almost before he knows it. . . .

There will be no abnormality in your growth if you follow this advice. Any concentration upon the vital centers, or even upon the development of certain powers, is injurious and is apt to lead to spiritual pride and black magic. If you seek to grow in Nature's way—for there is but one Law of Growth—whatever is within you will develop normally. Whatever you have earned as your own and have assimilated is yours by karmic right, hence growth means bringing this out, i.e. what you have really assimilated. The mustard seed grows into a mustard tree, with all its healing and medicinal qualities; the rose develops into the queen of all flowers, giving out its refreshing perfume—the symbol of love—to all. The spiritual lesson is that both grow and unfold by merely DOING THE DUTY THAT LIES NEAREST, that which is next at hand. They assimilate the earth-forces, the water, the air and the sun—go thou and do likewise.

Concentrate each day upon The Christ within. Hold fast to this main idea, that through the power of The Christ you can meet and conquer all that comes to you. Above all, learn to keep silent. "Dare, Do, Keep Silent" is the motto of this Order. The Master Jesus never talked of what He could do, but when the time came He simply did. Much force is wasted in words. The disciple needs to learn to concentrate his power in acts. If he talks he dissipates the power so that the act is feeble. Never say that you can do so and so, just GO AHEAD AND DO IT.

March 13th, 1908.

"I see myself in hell struggling for escape. It seems hopeless sometimes". . . .

Your condition and the struggle you are making, is under our watchful care. But, dear Brother, try to realize that when bound on the Wheel of Karma, to struggle but makes the cords cut deeper into your quivering flesh. Stop struggling. Lo! I say unto you: Peace, be still. All is well. Learn the lesson of saying, "Thy will be done," knowing that the will of the Father is victory, and that it will and must come. To think so much about your shortcomings and limitations is but to give them life and force; for thoughts are things and create after their kind. Determine to think strength, love and confidence until you draw them to you and build them into your life. If the evil does not at once fly away then persistently refuse to give it life. Do not recognize it. Repeat the little MORNING PRAYER each day and make it a living factor in your life. Rest in the positive belief that the love and help that you reach out for is yours for the taking. "Ask and ye shall receive."

July 6th, 1908.
"I have said much more than I intended to write, but if you know my motive and my desire you will understand why the words kept coming."

As to saying more than is wise in your letters to us, fear not to talk plainly to your Teacher; for only thus can you come into close touch. Words are sacred things though few there be who realize it. Words should be to thought what steam is to the engine; if directed to the cylinder and flywheel the engine does perfect work, but if the steam escapes through many tiny holes and cracks the power available for real work is diminished: and wasted steam, like idle words, is an indication of dissipated power. Man alone has the power to formulate thought into words. A parrot can imitate the sounds of words, but only man has reached the point of development where be is capable of rightly using this gift. It is a great responsibility. Every word we utter has not only its vibrations, but, together with the form, color and number of the letters composing it, possesses a potency that will never die, but go on and on through the ages until we, their creator, by the power of The Christ within, shall have redeemed them. Be their power for good or ill it forms one of the very considerable forces that go to make up the Law of Karma. It is one of those crops the sowing of which we are told we shall surely reap. Learn to value words as an index of thought. Make them your obedient servants. Do not waste them. Make every one count for something; for "For every idle word must thou give an account." Do not consider them idle, however, even if apparently trifling and foolish, provided they bring cheer and comfort into the life of some other. They are only idle when wasted in mere talking instead of doing.

Try to be as natural as possible in your dealing with your fellows. Never seem to claim for yourself any distinction above others, but hold fast within to the thought that the power of The Christ that worketh through you will never disappoint you or fail you.

May 23rd, 1908.

"I have not the constant capacity to see the Father in each experience in daily life. I am growing, however, and am determined to persevere, to make a living sacrifice of the self and learn how to transmute its forces. . . . I say sometimes I think like this, then am drawn back again into sense life and sink like a sodden leaf."

You have caught the idea and have clothed it and have created out of it an ideal. This is half the battle. You know that when a man tries to invent a thing or put into shape something which for a long time has lain dormant in his mind, an important step has been taken when he finds that he is able to think it all out in a practical way, and perhaps even make a sketch. After that the making of the model is not half so difficult. Therefore, make your ideal coherent and hold it fast. Build upon it, step by step, the Immortal Being which you know exists within yourself.

As to what you say about your lack of mental ability being an obstacle, we reply that, naturally, while the lower mind can never evolve into the spiritual mind, yet the lower mind has an important work to do in moulding and shaping the brain particles for the use of the Higher Self. In gaining the ability to grasp the highest vibrations the lower mind becomes a well trained servant to the Higher Self. It is therefore necessary to learn how to control and train the mind and cultivate the intellect; but it is well to bear in mind that the intellect is but the servant or tool for the mind to use. Moreover, intellectuality is not tested, as is generally supposed, by the amount of education one has had; for, while education does its work in training the lower mind, yet the mind once trained, and the brain built up into a fitting instrument for the use of the Higher Mind, it must then pass through an incarnation in which education—so-called book-learning—will be denied it, and conditions in life will make it impossible. The man or woman will be born into conditions where they will be forced by circumstances to forego what seems to be their rightful heritage. You often see this and remark, "So-and-so is so capable, yet he has never had more than a common-school education." Such an one would naturally look upon this as a great loss; but the fact is that, having had all opportunities for education in past lives, he has reached a point where the physical brain is to be moulded into an instrument to use along other lines, and therefore the old lines of thought are withheld. They are no longer needed by the Soul and it would be senseless to go on training the lower mind along them. If it is persisted in the man will become an intellectual machine, lacking in heart. Therefore, if the brain development has not gone hand in hand with the desire for spiritual advance, the incarnating Ego will select a vehicle and an environment in which everything, perhaps poverty, squalid surroundings, even sin, will tend to force the overcoming of obstacles, and in which the heart must be cultivated and the brain comparatively neglected. Such an incarnation successfully passed and conquered, the brain will be capable of being used by the Higher Self to a greater degree in accord with the capacity it has developed.

It is a fact that the Higher Self must have a perfect instrument if it is perfectly to record the Spiritual or Divine Mind upon the physical plane; for the Higher Self can only express itself through the instrument it possesses. Through an imperfect instrument the Higher Self can only register imperfectly, but this does not mean that a brain capable of less than perfect use is any great drawback; for many cultivate the love centers first. This, on the whole, is best; but before final liberation both must be coordinated.

Do not use the simile "like a sodden leaf," for no living Soul can ever become sodden, i.e. saturated with water (illusion). Such a condition could only come about in the most depraved, and only after the Higher Self had been forced to leave the personality to death and disintegration after it no longer contained a living Soul. Only after eons of purification could its particles again be given expression. . . .

The use of metaphors should be carefully chosen; for their meaning may be more far reaching than appears on the surface. You are never dead or sodden while containing one thought of love (life). You are but conscious of the ebb and flow of the spiritual force, and your feeling of depression is a perfectly natural result. It is but a consciousness of the out-breathing and the in-breathing of the Great Breath. At the out-breathing all is activity, while the in-drawing is a period of rest comparable to the night-time. Instead of allowing yourself to sink to the bottom of the stream, if you will hold the thought that it is but the night-time, and that you are calmly sleeping to recruit your strength and assimilate the spiritual force so that when the new day dawns you will be ready for new tasks, you will be strong and happy. In your study of the conditions of life and the trials that beset you, remember that the Soul must pass through, or be made to face, the depths of human degradation and emerge from them pure and unspotted. That is, after having gained a certain point in development the Soul must contact such conditions and prove itself capable of living in them without being of them, thus gaining mastery over them.

May 25th, 1908.

"I have an 85-year-old father, and bad men have got their hands on his property and mine, and I struggle to get into such condition that he will have a home and plenty. I pray, hope and battle and toil almost night and day; for father is one of earth's angels who has labored all his life in doing good. My work to keep the home nice, to care for him and to attend to business leaves me not a moment I can call my own."

No matter what the burden laid upon you, it is not laid there merely that you may suffer, nor does any God wish you to bear it. It is yours because somehow, somewhere, sometime you missed a lesson in life that only this heavy burden could teach you. Therefore, conditions worked together and you were brought face to face with your lesson. Try to realize this. Then, if you can admit that what you are forced to bear is merely meant as a lesson to point out some shortcoming or absolute fault, know well that the moment you LEARN THE LESSON or correct the fault the experience will no longer be needed and it will pass away. Perhaps you lack faith or patience or love, or you are given to the love of money; for we do not have to be rich to love money, there are many more poor than rich who love it. No one but yourself can put a finger on the sore spot; but when once you have found it go to work diligently, with all your heart, to correct the fault.

Rest sure in the love of your Father-in-heaven who has said that "Not one of these little ones shall perish," No matter how little you are in your own mind, after you have scraped off the barnacles that are sinking you beneath the waters, no matter how heavy your burden, your Heavenly Father (who is your own Higher Self) will not let you perish. He will take away the lesson as soon as it is learned and will give you another which may require better physical conditions.

May 17th, 1908.

"I am sure that I am growing, yet have experienced much darkness. I try to believe, I do believe, that the darkness is just as natural as the light to the growing plant. . . . This self, the Watcher of the Threshold, I find a terrible monster, and seemingly, all but impossible to overcome. Yet while the fight goes on am slowly learning to say and live the words, 'Thy will be done'."

You should not think of the darkness even as a night, or as a trial, but as a necessary condition for growth. The seed will never take root unless it is buried in the darkness of the earth. If you could penetrate the consciousness of a growing plant you would find that, while it spends a time blindly searching for light, sending out strong, firm roots hunting here and there in the dark earth, there will come a time later on when it will have gathered the consciousness necessary to send up its sprout into the light. It will then recognize that the period of darkness was the most important step; for without good, firm roots it would be withered by the sunshine; yet the sunshine was what it was seeking all the time. While the seed was still down in the darkness of the earth it was the same sun that was giving it life and power and drawing its sprout upward to the light while it was still mercifully shielded by the earth from the too strong beams of the light itself.

You are often told to live close to Nature, yet very few understand the significance of that injunction. It does not necessarily mean living in a tent or sleeping on the ground; but it does mean correlating your consciousness with Nature, trying through meditation to enter into the phases of natural growth and development, recognizing the similarity and the oneness of all growth. In Nature you will find an explanation of every experience through which you pass. The man who has learned the great lesson of resting on the bosom of the Great Mother, Nature, and breathing in unison with her, pulsating with her heart-beats, is the one who lives close to Nature, no matter whether he is in the midst of the whirling business life of a great city or dwells, as Cowper puts it, in "A lodge in some vast wilderness, far from the evil haunts of men."

Learn the lesson of living close to Nature and you will find that the Dweller, whom you have confused with the Watcher or Guardian—the Guardian being something entirely different—will be no more to you than are the cold winter blasts and other material enemies of growth that are conquered not by fighting them, but by a persistent drawing to yourself of the Life Eternal out of the very elements of discord. Nothing in the nature of man is inherently evil; it is only evil through its misuse, and the evils that are attached to it. Determine to deliver it from evil, and to find The Christ force within EVERY temptation and everything that assails you, knowing full well that these things are the portion of goods that have been given you by your Father at your request—your just belongings that you have deserved and out of which you must create your immortal habitation. Not one thing must be lost or wasted or destroyed; but each must be transmuted and its golden potency indrawn and built into the immortal Temple of the Living Christ. This is the meaning of the sentence in the Lord's Prayer, "deliver us from evil."

May 30th, 1908.

"Am surprised to find myself in the 4th Degree. Was it due to my number of evolution, and if so how was it determined? So many writers assert 'I am God. I am That I am.' I cannot grasp their meaning."

You are in the 4th Degree because you have reached that point in evolution. That is, you have reached the point where you have the conscious desire to seek for Wisdom and are feeling around for some guiding hand to point out The Path. In this you have fulfilled the first requirement of the Law, "Seek and ye shall find; knock and it shall be opened unto you." Therefore do not be surprised that the cry of your heart has found listening ears, or that the hand you sought is touching yours.

The "I" is the Higher Self, the overshadowing Father-in-heaven. It is the True Self in that it is the Ego—a Spark of the Infinite—incarnating again and again in an animal body for the purpose of gaining experience in matter and, through its informing physical atoms in an earthly body, to help redeem (spiritualize) matter. The whole body and its organs is but an ephemeral, transitory conglomeration of atoms, created and gathered together by the Real Self to use as a vehicle very much as a man might make or create a garment to wear for a certain purpose and for a certain time. The body wears out and is cast aside just as the garment is, and a new one put on; but the Self never changes. It gains more experience and needs a better garment from time to time until, finally, it masters the matter which makes up its physical garments and immortalizes it so that the personality is swallowed up in the Individuality; the mortal puts on immortality and becomes one with its Father-in-heaven. The animal body, however, has a consciousness of its own which is always striving to rule the organism instead of the Higher Self. Until the Higher Self has gained full control it is often trampled under foot and The Christ force crucified. When passion and desire, with the bit in their teeth, dash the personality recklessly down the hill of sensual pleasures, disease and death naturally result; but the moment the Real Self asserts its prerogatives and grasps the reins the personality will become the useful servant, and passion and desire, not killed out but controlled, will trot quietly along in the harness of service, obedient to the Master's will.

The Ego may be looked upon as the Soul, while the Spirit is the overshadowing Divinity. As we have said before, the Soul is a Spark from the Infinite, while the Spirit is the Flame. The Spirit is the Breath of the Absolute; it has no individuality. Just as you might light a thousand candles with the same flame without detracting from it, yet each new flame would be individualized, so with Souls. Souls are all Sparks of the One Flame.

May 12th, 1908.

"I am a member of the Society and it is no doubt very presumptuous in me to feel dissatisfied so soon. I have been a member only about a year and a half but I feel restless yet I am devoted to the teachings."

All teachings that bring to humanity a knowledge of the higher truths and that awaken an interest in spiritual development are useful; but individual Souls need special lines of instruction. Some find help under one teacher, some under another, and if your Higher Self knows that the one from whom you are striving to learn is not the most helpful one for you, you will be impressed with a feeling of dissatisfaction. Yet this does not mean that the teachings you have been receiving are not excellent for a certain stage of growth and just what you needed at one time. The great lesson to learn is to follow the leadings of your Higher Self and take for yourself what appeals to you and helps you. But be just as ready to concede to others the right to choose for themselves. Try to realize that they too have the guidance of their Higher Self, and if they are receiving help from any source that is the step needed by them at that time.

If at any time you feel dissatisfied with the teachings received from this source you must apply the same rule. That which you need will appeal to you. One thing may appeal to you today and in a month or a year you may grow away from it. If you are sincere and earnest, this merely indicates that you have learned one lesson and must look elsewhere for the next. For this reason no lasting vows should ever be given or required. The only vow that a Neophyte can give is one to his Higher Self to follow unfalteringly wherever the Star of Initiation leads. No earthly teacher can ever take him more than a step along The Path; but his own Higher Self will guide him all the way if he only listens to the Still Small Voice.

May 7th, 1908.

"You spoke of certain stages where the neophyte could not be helped by teachers, etc. Will you please explain?. . . . The thought of a student class is undoubtedly most laudable but I must meet its leaders and know more of their personnel and that of the members before feeling assured that affiliation is the right step for me. I want to study with those who possess a clear insight and through whom my growth may be accelerated, not impeded."

A student is never left to stumble along alone; for the unseen Helpers are always near to guide and direct. But there are times when certain characters need to be left alone, not to themselves, but to their unseen Teachers. They need to seek and find in The Silence the Truth. Only when they have done this are they ready to accept it when presented outwardly. If they are over-fed with outer help, so-called; told to do this or that, it only upsets them and retards their progress. Generally the rough and thorny way of struggle and sorrow is due to a lack of realization that within each earnest heart there is The Christ center, and that "I (the Christ within) am the Way, the Truth and the Life: no man cometh unto the Father, but by me," i.e. through the revealed Christ-power within.

Having found within your own heart a well-spring of love and faith and life, it is not of much moment who or what your co-laborers in the class are; for YOU come to bring the Light that YOU have found within to share with them. Once found nothing can dim that Light, and it does not matter if the personalities of the members do not meet your expectations—perhaps you do not meet theirs for YOU know that you are not dealing with the outer personalities, but that YOU can see beyond into the heart of each. If you go with this attitude the divine Light of The Christos will spread from heart to heart, and all will be benefited by your presence. Remember that you do not go merely to acquire knowledge for yourself alone and give nothing in return. . . . If you cannot put your thoughts into words and enter into the discussion of the lesson, you can nevertheless fill the room with loving and helpful thoughts and give encouragement and help to the faithful ones who are trying to help you, even though, like yourself, they feel that they have much to learn.

"During the past two years have been passing through a condition of darkness, sorrow and pain, as though much of the past were being forced upon me. Why is this?"

Your condition of spiritual darkness is the result of a natural law pertaining to spiritual development. When the neophyte starts out in earnest to become a disciple the first thing that happens is that, by the very effort to separate from the world, he becomes more sensitive and the world's conditions press more heavily upon him. Also, the Karma that might under the old conditions, be spread out over many years, or even lives, is willingly taken up by the Soul; for it has determined to overcome. Whether the personality is aware of it or not, the Soul or Higher Self has consciously taken upon itself the redeeming of all the old mistakes NOW, AT ONCE. Nearly always the first effect of any decided step along The Path is depressing. A recognition of the world's misery weighs upon the sensitive consciousness and a great loneliness and helplessness surrounds the disciple, because he has separated from the old and has not yet made conscious correlation with the new. He has answered the call "Come ye out, and be ye separate," yet he has not realized the inner peace or felt the loving compassion of his Guide and Savior, his True Self.

It is this experience which is symbolized by the death and burial and the lying in the grave for three days. The three days do not refer to any period of time; for you lie in the grave until the completion of three periods which, for convenience, we will call sunrises. The Sun of Righteousness must rise for you upon three days or conditions. First, it must illumine your understanding. It must penetrate into the grave of despondency and loss of hope and show you why you are dead and buried. Second, it must illumine your consciousness so that the realization of your Father's nearness and guidance shall become a reality. Then the grave, with all its horrors will become endurable; for you know that you must pass through this experience ere the new life can begin. As St. John puts it (XII-24): "Except a corn of wheat fall into the ground and die, it abideth alone: but if it die, it bringeth forth much fruit." You realize that you must lie there without struggling or complaining, just as the grain does, until the Spirit working in you can bring you forth anew. Third, the Sun of Righteousness must illumine your heart. That is, the love that passeth understanding must dawn within you so that you can love all things, all men, and all conditions, and be able to cry out, "O death, where is thy sting? O grave, where is thy victory?" On the third day, very early in the morning, ye shall rise from the grave and become a Child of the Resurrection. Remember that the days, like the days of creation, each have their morning, their noontide and their evening; and it was very early in the morning of the THIRD day, ere it was yet light, that The Christ arose from the tomb.

There is a wonderful significance in the expression "very early in the morning" that will be referred to in our lesson on EARTH'S FINER FORCES. Until you receive that lesson we trust this short explanation of why you are passing through such darkness will give you strength to lie quietly in the grave, in loving trust, until the morning of the THIRD day dawns for you and the Spirit brings you forth anew.

In your case you have been learning some very deep lessons and must have time to digest them and correlate them with your life. For until you have been tried and have proven your strength you cannot bring forth the harvest. The greater the work laid out for a neophyte, the greater the necessity for thorough testing. This is a merciful law, for the suffering and evil Karma would be much worse to bear if you were given a great opportunity and failed for lack of proper training; for, of necessity, you would draw others down with you. One by one the things that hold you back are being taken from you, and your whole character is being tested and tried. Fight on, brave Soul. You have our love, our help and our encouragement.

May 19th, 1908.

"I have been exceedingly busy as I am employed in a hardware store. . . . and it keeps me busy so that when night comes I am worn out so that it is very difficult to concentrate and gather my thoughts. . . . I long to know, but at present I cannot as I am under this strain, but I am hoping that I shall soon be in a position where all is peaceful and quiet."

So many students are in a position similar to yours, so busy that everything but bread-and-butter winning seems crowded out. This is partly the result of the false standards of business and the methods which give no chance for the poor man to get ahead, because the man with money is king. But behind it all there is a Karma working itself out collectively in the masses of humanity, and individually in its units. No man is in the wrong place. This does not mean that the man who finds himself in the position of under-dog should not try to better himself. There is only one way to effectually bring about a better condition, and that is for him to recognize that he is where he is because the Soul, or Higher Self, realizes that there is some important lesson to learn which those conditions can teach better than any other, and set to work to learn that lesson. No mental or faith-cure for poverty can in reality lift him out of his condition. It can, if applied to the exclusion of all other desires, bring him riches for a time; that is, if he is willing to give up learning the lesson which his Higher Self has set for him to learn and for which the path of his present incarnation was especially mapped out, and devotes his whole desire to obtaining wealth. He will get it, but he will have to come back and learn the lesson, perhaps at a time when the learning will be far harder.

You are beginning to realize that conditions do not really retard, but are intended to make you THINK and take account of stock. First, try to determine what lesson you must learn, then take it determinedly to heart until you have conquered. The world's Karma limits individual Karma; but within those limits individual Karma places you either high or low. We desire to help each student to live the best he can in his karmic position, and to help him understand himself so that he can use this earth life as a stepping-stone to something higher. We do not desire impossibilities. We know that no man has conditions given to him that he does not need, and that the moment he gets out of a condition its highest good he is rid of it forever. We aim to help all to find the Jewel of Truth in the mire of their existence, and to make their lives more tolerable because less mysterious and crushing. Nothing that we understand can crush or terrify us; for we can set out to overcome it without fear. You may remember the story of the great naturalist who, while watching a butterfly emerge from its chrysalis, was moved to cut some of the confining sheath by pity at its violent struggles to free itself. But when the butterfly emerged he found it but a poor, weak, crippled thing unable to fly. He was forced to see that the very violence of the struggle for freedom was necessary for the perfection of its strength and self-reliance. It is just so with each human Soul in its struggle to free itself from the chrysalis of the physical. The greater the struggle, if persisted in to victory, the stronger and more selfreliant will be the new-born Soul.

March 6th, 1908.

"But in the existence of free will can you show me that it exists to any considerable degree? I know that it is the teaching of both secularists and occultists, but in its application to life I have yet to learn its range of action. I do not, and cannot, philosophically, believe in the final loss of a single spark of divinity—yet—if free-will existed such a loss follows as a matter of course. Is it free, or free within limits?"

As to free-will, each and every Soul is but a separated part of the One Life, and as such its highest aspect has but the Will of the Father, i.e. to do His will on earth in a separated body as it is done in the bosom of the Father. As it gets more and more immersed in matter the True Self sets up many side issues as it were (see lesson on REINCARNATION); makes many new karmic debts. And while the True Self never changes in its desire and will to be reunited to the Father, yet the lower or animal consciousness (the sum of the consciousness of the atoms composing the various bodies through which the Soul has garnered experience) has set up a will of its own. This has crystallized into an entity with a will opposed to the Will of the Real Self. This lower will is not free, for it can, and indeed must, ultimately, be subservient to the Will of the Real Self.

But perhaps this does not answer your question; for probably what you mean by free-will is freedom of choice as to the guidance of the environments and experiences of life. But, my son, in this case as in the former, there is absolute free-will for the Real Self. For, as I have said, being a separated part of the whole, the desire is to gain such experiences as shall fit it to fill the place which is its own in the Temple of Truth. At each incarnation the Soul chooses such an expression in the earth life as shall give the best opportunity to gain the needed knowledge. The Soul will not that the perishable mortal body of flesh shall skim gaily through its allotted time; for only too well does the Soul know the dangers of such care-free lives and the depressing lines of Karma that result, and which must be worked out ere it can go on with other needed experiences; it wills to suffer and conquer and learn. After the result of each petty life-period is garnered the Soul creates a new path in which to walk, perhaps even more strenuous than those already traversed. The Soul sees what is needed to impress the most important lessons upon the true consciousness; for the Soul never has experiences that are not needed. It wills to learn, and when the lesson is learned and the experience assimilated, it wills to experience something else; and so on and on, until a consciousness of ALL conditions on the earth plane is garnered into the storehouse of the Real Self.

April 13th, 1908.

"I find myself so much out of touch with the community here who are thoroughly saturated with church dogmas regarding forgiveness of sins and reducing Deity to physical plane dimensions that it would be very selfish in me to wish the gap made wider. I am doing what little I can to assist some to a larger conception without producing chaos in their minds."

All manifestations of life, from atom to cosmos, are in a circle. This is as true of the spiritual life-wave of a community as of any of the lower forms of life. You feel that because you have some conception of truth in advance of your neighbors that you are separated from them, and you fear to take another step lest the separation grow wider. I know your difficulty is a real one, and that from your standpoint you do not see that there is extreme egotism in the supposition that you are so far in advance that in kindness and condescension you will not make the gap wider. Just for a moment try to grasp the idea of a circle with you and your neighbors disposed in various positions on its outer rim. Naturally, as you cannot see around the circle, the man at the opposite pole seems hopelessly separated from you. But if you will consider the manifestations of life you will find that within the circle of manifestation there is a germinal point or nucleus, and that from this central point all growth proceeds; that the radiating lines of force spread out and touch all points of the circumference at the same time. Therefore, any nutriment or knowledge—no matter of what type—applied to one point would be gradually absorbed by the germinal point, and from thence would radiate to all parts of the circle. A community is just such a circle. Its thought and spiritual ideas have crystallized and have poured their force into the germinal point, and that point can give out only such food as corresponds with the stimulus from the outer rim demanding a certain kind of response. If any point on the circle should open its consciousness to a higher rate of vibration or correlate with more advanced truth, i.e. should live The Christ life, the absolute Law of Harmony must advance all the rest, even without a word being spoken, that is, IF THE TRUTH RECEIVED IS ASSIMILATED AND EXPRESSED IN THE LIFE as vital growth. You must "live the life."

The very truth of the conditions you so much deplore shows that there is a hunger, a reaching out for light. All true growth proceeds from the center. What comes from the heart touches the heart. No one can give spiritual force to another until he has made it a part of himself; for as long as the "great heresy of separateness" holds sway over your mind you are in bondage to the lower self. Find the center within your own heart and you will soon find that you are closer to all humanity, rather than more separate. If your object is merely to be considered a saint, then failure and sorrow is your inevitable portion.

June 1st, 1908.

"Your communication of nearly a month ago has been very carefully considered, ... and I have waited for the outcome and believe that the leading of the Higher Self has prompted me to take up the work of the Order. Upon my suggestion. . . . wrote you. . . . and we may find others to join us, but until then we would like to think of ourselves as a little nucleus, a little attracting center, working for the development of the best within ourselves and humanity."

We appreciate your attitude of devotion to the Higher Life, and we are glad that you have realized the only way really to help humanity is to take hold of that morsel of humanity over which you have been given command, (your various bodies and all pertaining to them, the portion of goods belonging to you—given to you by your Father ere you took your journey into this far country of earth life) and begin by redeeming it. That is the only way to make an impression and help accomplish the work. If we try to lift up the whole mass we are crushed under its weight and become hopelessly discouraged by the vastness of the task. It is like trying to break a great bundle of twigs all at once. But, to find, as a Soul reality, that the "I and my brother are one" and then set to work within the Self to seek and to save that which is lost, is to create a center or home in which The Christ can manifest—a fit Temple for the Living God (your Higher Self) to dwell in among men.

This is the sure, in fact the only true way, to become an agent of the Masters. We are apt to speak lightly, or at least without understanding, of the body as the Temple of the Living God, but a few moments meditation on the subject each day will open up wonderous vistas of The Path to Mastery. A Holy Temple must not only have its sacred shrine wherein The Presence dwelleth; but it must also have its attendant High Priest and High Priestess, its daily sacrifice, its feasts and its fasts of purification; and over and above all, it must make its impression upon the community. Think back over the ages and see how the rise and fall of civilizations has followed the purity or the pollution of the Temples and the worship. Enumerate them and you will find an exact analogy to the effect on a community of one purified human temple with its worship of the Living God, be it in apparently ever so humble an human body. When two or three such are gathered together the promise must fulfill itself: "Behold, there am I (The Christos) in the midst."

Jan. 21st, 1908.

"Will you kindly tell me whether this philosophy will reveal to me why there seems to be so much demand for self-sacrifice with apparently so little return?"

This philosophy will at least show you what the Real Self is. And once you become acquainted with, or even begin to realize, your Real Self you will know that there can be no self-sacrifice. All lower forms of self are but expressions of the One Self, and must be indrawn into the One Self. The lower selves are like the outer husks of the seed which are dissolved and their substance indrawn to form nourishment for the seed, to enrich it and enable it to grow and blossom. If you choose to call promoting the growth and blossoming in that way self-sacrifice, it must remain that for you for the present. But if you call it growth and unfoldment, the return is happiness and a greater fulness of life.

May 5th, 1908.
"I hesitate to take a step which may place me in the light of an example, lest I fail in some way that would bring reproach upon the work."

As to failings, we all have them. The greatest example the world can have is to see a brave Soul struggling to do right. A perfect man — perfect in his own estimation — if such an one could be found, perfect and immaculately moral and correct in every outward seeming, would help the world very little. It is those who are honest with themselves; who know their own weaknesses yet are striving to conquer; who recognize that they are not above their fellow men; who are capable of feeling a sympathetic thrill with every failing and can grasp a brother's hand and from the heart encourage him to struggle onward, because they themselves are still struggling; they are the ones who are the real examples. Apply this test to any earthly contest and you will see that it is not the one who is perfect, who knows it all, who helps; but it is the one who is struggling with all his strength for supremacy who awakens the spirit of endeavor in his comrades.

June 15th, 1908.
"I am becoming unpleasantly sensitive to all conditions; today I am on the heights and tomorrow in the depths of despair and misery. Can you tell me how to gain more poise?"

Poise is not the stoical indifference to pain and pleasure; but rather rising above it. We never reach a point where the waves of force generated by the opposite poles, pain and pleasure, cannot reach us; but we can rise above them so they cannot sweep us from one extreme to another. It is like riding on a see-saw: those on the ends are lifted now high in the air and now are bumped on the ground; but a person standing in the middle and balancing it has absolute control of both extremities without being moved to any appreciable extent in either direction. To enjoy intensely carries with it, as the opposite swing of the pendulum, the power to suffer to a corresponding degree. Poise is the ability to remain calm at the center, and, while recognizing and understanding both the greatest joy and the greatest sorrow, not be carried to either extreme.

Ere a disciple can conquer he must become more than ordinarily sensitive; must be capable of vibrating more intensely than his imagination can picture at lower stages of development. No Soul can enter into the joy of the Lord, i.e. have an illuminating sense of the glory of The Christos, until that Soul has become like a quivering bundle of nerves, capable of registering the extremes of sensation. But with this extreme sensitiveness must come the power to control it; the ability to hold still and not be moved; in fact, to master sensation. To control sensation is the first step toward Mastery. Until this step has been taken all others are barred by the very laws of Nature; for the seat of sensation is in the astral body which is the path of communication between the physical and the spiritual. Hence, until the Soul can consciously walk this path without fear and without reproach, steady and calm, the disciple can never reach into the spiritual realms.

You can gain a good idea of what we mean if you will study the needle of a compass that is badly poised (centered). Such a needle is called "sluggish," that is, it is not easily set in motion; but when it is it rushes madly around the circle and probably gets wedged or stuck. At most it will fail to settle on the N point. A highly sensitized needle, on the contrary, will register every magnetic wave and will be in almost a constant quiver; but no matter how rapid the vibration caused by adverse conditions, it will scarcely move from the N point. If it should be displaced it will always come back and settle exactly true to the North. This, in a nut-shell, is the whole lesson of poise.

April 21st, 1908.

"I have never been able to see how 'a ray from the infinite' can in its essence be separated from the all-pervading whole and require any working out of its own redemption. To me the working out of a personal salvation partakes of the nature of selfishness which is the principal cause of present world troubles."

In answer to your query let me give you a parable. Two men were ship-wrecked in the night while they slept, and were cast upon a desert island. One, upon gaining consciousness, was very much concerned as to how he got there, so he spent his time sitting around trying to solve the problem. The other man was just as much puzzled; but instead of sitting down to think it out, he started at once to find out what kind of an island he had landed upon and how he was going to live there most comfortably. He was so busy with this that he had very little time to worry about how he got there. He built a hut, found food and water, and finally discovered a mine of pure gold. He also found a means of signalling and making his distress known. In the fulness of time a ship saw his signals and took him home to civilization. There he found out all about how he got on the island where he had learned so many valuable lessons; and, moreover, he was very rich. He then realized that his experience on the island was for his best good after all, even though he could not see it at the time.

The other man pined away and died in hunger and misery because he could not solve the problem of how he got on the island. Which of these men think you, was the wiser? He who made the best of things, using all the powers and intelligence he had and waiting until he got to a point where knowledge of the "why" was possible, or he who made himself miserable because he wanted knowledge that could not be given him until he himself had found a way to reach the necessary point?

Thus must it be with mankind. Solve the problems that confront you here and now and the higher problems that belong to the Infinite leave until your finite mind becomes absorbed into the Infinite, when all things will be made plain.

When it is once grasped that the working out of a personal salvation is the only way really to help the world, the man who neglects it is a retarder of the public good. No one can be a savior until he has redeemed every atom of all the bodies, (physical, mental and spiritual) committed to his care. These are the portion of goods belonging to him — given to him at his own request by his Father-in-heaven ere he took his long journey into this "far country" of physical embodiment. If one fails to see the necessity for caring for and redeeming his goods, he must eat husks with the swine until he is ready to say: "I will arise and go to my Father."

You say you are willing to take light from any source; then look for the light of The Christ that shines within your own heart. Dig among the refuse and uncover the Flame and set it upon a candlestick that the light may shine before men.

Jan. 9th, 1908.

"I feel the need of guidance and protection in treading the narrow path between subjective mediumship on the one hand and 'quenching of the spirit' on the other. I have had dreams and visions of a marked character, some of which seem like initiations. Also some psychic experiences. . . . I have never had from anyone an explanation of them, or personal instruction in these matters."

I would like you to write down carefully just what your brain mind was able to register of the initiations through which you seem to have passed. You have realized the truth that it is, indeed, a narrow path between subjective mediumship and the "quenching of the spirit." This is the "Bridge of Swords" over which Mahomet crossed the abyss ere he entered paradise. Every true disciple of the Masters of Wisdom must walk this path. There is no other bridge across that terrible abyss; but each of the Masters has crossed it and They are waiting with loving encouragement on the other side. They have fastened a three-fold cord all the way across. Hold fast to it and your feet will not slip in the darkness, nor will the monsters of the deep have power to frighten you. This three-fold cord is Love, Trust and Obedience. Your loving Father waits patiently for you on the brink and sends out His voice to you through the darkness; a still small voice, yet it sounds in your heart like the sound of many waters. If you listen it will swallow up all other sounds and will say to you, "Lo! I am with thee, even unto the end. Fear thou not!" But, dear child, full well do we know the way is lonely and your human heart cries out for companionship. You have reached a point where you shall meet and know your fellow travelers on The Path. Therefore I say unto thee: Open thine understanding and heed the words I have spoken. Follow the dictates of your intuition; for no matter if your earthly brain does forget, your Soul KNOWS and can make no mistake.

In the early days of the Theosophical movement it was necessary to warn disciples against psychicism because of the many dangers that beset the way, knowing full well that THE REAL MYSTIC could not be quenched. Unfortunately, however, these well meant warnings were so embellished by the later followers of H. P. B. . . . . by those who knew least about such experiences and who became most rabid and bitter against anyone who apparently took a step beyond their own dense, materialistic ideas that there was great danger of 'quenching of the spirit'. This is one of the reasons for this Movement, namely, that all who are able to perceive spiritually may have the personal help necessary in treading the "Bridge of Swords."

Spiritual Growth and Development 127

March 3rd, 1908.
"How can I increase my love for my 'fellow man?' when the very sight of some of them gives me the 'creeps'? Now I do not mean the unfortunates. I do seem to love the outcast, the tramp, the generally unlovely! But people of refinement, even one member of my own family, I just dread to hear her footstep and dislike her personality so that I could almost scream when I hear her coming. Many a time I go out of the house and stay out as long as I can just to avoid looking at her. I feel condemned."

As to what you say about increasing your love for your fellow man, the best way is to forget all about those who upset you and think only of The Christ love and draw near to that. Keep away from those who are absolutely repugnant to you if possible; for there is always a good reason. If you think continually of those who only arouse the evil side of your nature you retard your growth, and most likely increase their natural antagonism. If you cannot do this, determine that you will create a wall of force around yourself that nothing inharmonious or unlovely can pierce; that you will not speak an unkind word; that you are too well balanced and surrounded with immortal love to allow anything that is outside to affect you. Repeat the HEALING PRAYER and realize that you ARE filled with "Life and Love and Purity," and that you will give out nothing but those forces to anyone with whom you come in contact.

If anything inharmonious arises, be sure that it is something outside yourself, then calmly ignore it. Generally there is some condition brought over from a past life that must be worked out in your present environment. If you realize that you will have to endure until you learn the lesson of equanimity and grow above their power to disquiet, you will at once find an improvement. It has been said that people are neither our friends nor our enemies, only our teachers; and we may make things worse by trying to force conditions instead of learning the lesson they have to teach. Hold the attitude of always being ready to help whenever your help is needed.

July 25th
"I am a member of a New Thought Church and the classes and teachings of the same. . . . I have done some teaching along New Thought lines and am considered very advanced and strong by my associates there. . . . During the last year. . . . I seem to have no vitality or enthusiasm over anything. I first thought it was a physical condition, but physical

remedies do not abolish it. Besides, for many years now my mind has been able to make me forget and overcome my body. My mind seems to be unable to give me the stimulus it used to. I have to constantly fight depression. There are no material causes for this mental heaviness. . . . Perhaps you may think it is a case of mental indigestion, but I have tried rest for my mind, but it only makes these attacks of numbness more pronounced. Is there any knowledge which can help me?"

You ask for help and the Law is that all who ask must receive; but we feel that we cannot help you much without upsetting some of your preconceived ideas, and we know from sad experience that this is not a pleasant task. But when one asks we can but give the food the Master has given us to distribute. It is but two loaves of bread and five small fishes, and those who cannot eat bread and fish may have to go away hungry; but for those who can eat and be filled with such food they are more than welcome.

You complain of a lack of vitality and enthusiasm; let us look for the cause. The whole trend of the so-called New Thought is to deify mind, to make mind supreme. As you put it, the mind has been trained to forget and overcome the body. That is all very well, BUT what if the mind itself grows exhausted? What if it reaches a point of development where it has emptied itself? Where constant affirmations and strenuous thought forces have ceased to satisfy? where the mind refuses longer to sit upon the throne it has usurped? where the mind has awakened to a knowledge that it is but a vehicle, a servant, and cries out for help and guidance? This is the point that you have reached, and nothing can help you but a recognition of this truth.

Instead of bowing down to mind, listen for the Still Small Voice that speaks in the "Soundless sound." What was it that led you to come to us for help? Whatever it was listen to it again and ask it if this advice is good. You are hungry for Divine Love and the guidance of your Father-in-heaven. You have reached the parting of the ways and must choose the table from which you will eat henceforth. If the morsel of food you receive herewith is acceptable to you we would be pleased to hear the reply you receive from the Voice.

July 28th

"Do you not regard mind as God's greatest gift to man, and the desire to cultivate it a divine instinct?. . . . I feel like a chrysalis—in a state of development—so reach out to the light wherever I see a glimpse."

As to mind being God's greatest gift, we would say that mind is, indeed, man's crowning gift, or, to put it differently, mind is the highest step attainable for mere man. But mind or Manas, the fifth principle, is dual and is called in Eastern philosophy the higher and lower Manas. It can be attached to the lower principles (Sthula Sharira or gross physical body; Linga Sharira or astral body or body of sensation; Prana or life-force, and Kama or animal soul) and make man an intellectual animal, or it can be drawn upward and merged into and become one with the higher principles (Buddhi, the Soul and Atma, the Spirit) and form the Divine triangle—something more than mere human mind. Mind alone is but an instrument, a tool; but mind merged into Soul and Spiritual essence becomes the Divine Indweller, the Father-in-heaven, the Higher Self. In the majority of mankind mind is vacillating, occasionally reaching up to the Divine, but again falling to earth.

To devote all one's effort to the cultivation of mind (the instrument) and to set mind upon the throne of Spirit, is eventually to become a mere intellectual machine; and sooner or later the mind itself rebels and forces rest and recuperation. To quote Bulwer Lytton: "The soul has need of pauses of repose,—intervals of escape, not only from the flesh, but even from the mind. A man of loftiest intellect will experience times when mere intellect not only fatigues him, but amidst its most original conceptions, amidst its proudest triumphs, has a something trite and commonplace compared with one of those vague intimations of a spiritual destiny which are not within the ordinary domain of reason." We strongly recommend you to read Bulwer Lytton's A STRANGE STORY. Read it carefully, recognizing that the character, Dr. Fenwick, represents mind or pure intellect and reason alone; Margrave animal man alone, and Lillian the Soul, and we think you will get a new conception of the relative position and value of the three.

What you are pleased to term "instinct" as prompting you to write to us we would give the higher name of intuition. Instinct is that which guides the lower kingdoms alone, not man. Instinct is that unseen guiding force of the universal Life-essence that urges inanimate nature to seek for the best conditions for growth, and to overcome obstacles and adapt itself to conditions until it reaches the end for which it was created. It also acts in all creatures, animal man included, with an incessant urge toward an end,—the end for which they are destined. Intuition, on the contrary, is the Voice of the Soul speaking to man, who alone of all creation has reached a point in evolution where mind has become dual; for many brutes have mind, and a highly developed mind, but it is not dual. That is, the brutes have only what we call lower Manas and are guided through instinct by the Universal Mind, while man, who has reached the point of development where the lower mind has been overshadowed by and attached to Soul and Spirit, has the guidance put into his own hands. Hence, the brute thinks; but only along lines which lead to its own wellbeing. Man can listen to the dictates of a higher Will and can fashion his mind after the Divine, or we might put it that the brute is guided by an Universal Mind outside of itself while man has his source of guidance within himself and is individually responsible for the result.

The chrysalis which you feel enfolding you is the effort of the mind to draw away from the lower fields of mere intellectual activity, and the struggling into the Divine Light where the mind shall take its true place at the base of the triangle whose apex is Divinity. Just as a grub, when it has fulfilled its life as a grub and has garnered all the experience to be gained from that state, wraps itself round with a cocoon and becomes a chrysalis and drops into a lethargic sleep only to awaken as a butterfly,—a thing with wings capable of reaching up into and exploring a higher element (the air),—so the mind shall find its wings and shall soar upward into spiritual realms. The grub and the butterfly are the same creature, but how different! The butterfly has not left the earth, but it is no longer confined to it. So it is with the mind when wedded to Soul and guided by intuition.

To laboriously cultivate the mind is well, for knowledge is power; but there is a better way, the way indicated by the great Master Jesus when, in speaking of The Christ principle within, He said: "I am the way, the truth and the life." For Christ-life is Wisdom, and Wisdom includes all knowledge. When The Christ within is enthroned the Still Small Voice will never desert or fail us, and ONLY THEN are all things ours, all knowledge and all needed help; for your Father knoweth that he have need of them be they what they may. The attempt to avoid living The Christ-life by worshiping mind is futile. "Seek ye first the kingdom of heaven and all these things shall be added unto you" is not a mere platitude, but the most practical of all occult directions.

Feb. 2nd, 1908.

"I should be glad if you could give me a clear explanation of how I should approach the 'entering into the silence.' I have been attempting this but the result so far has only been to disturb my usual sound sleep and bringing into my waking consciousness broken remnants of life during sleep, many of which I can only associate with the working of the lower mind. Also what will the remembering consist of and when is the best time to make the effort? So far it has been made immediately before going to sleep."

All that is desirable at the time of falling to sleep is to compose the mind and give an upward trend to the thoughts by a heart-felt prayer such as we sent you with the last lesson, (the MORNING PRAYER. Ed.). Sink off to sleep as nearly as possible like a little child, with a calm faith in the Father's care and a feeling of brotherhood to all humanity. Should there be anyone with whom you find it hard to get along, or who has deeply wronged you, do not harass yourself in a vain effort to think lovingly of them. Just say: "I forgive. If I cannot forgive now I pray the Father to give me a forgiving spirit." In the meantime put the unforgiven one out of your mind entirely; for man cannot think of wrongs without stirring up unkind feelings, and this must never be allowed, especially upon going to sleep.

The time to enter into The Silence is any convenient time when you can have at least ten minutes alone. If possible, have the same time, the same room and the same chair; for thought impresses itself upon so-called inanimate things and in this way no effort is lost. Sit down comfortably, close your eyes and, after repeating the PRAYER OF CONSECRATION[1] and adding any personal petition that your Soul dictates, quietly determine that the mind shall remain blank. Then BELIEVE that your Real Self can and will draw near and will guide you if you can succeed in stilling the physical vibrations. This may take time and practice, and you may fall asleep; but do not let anything discourage or worry you. If your mind wanders or becomes active, bring it back and mentally repeat: Silence! Silence! You will soon find that you will come from this period of silence refreshed in body and mind, and that you have strong impressions and a comprehension of truths that

---

[1] See Appendix.

previously were vague. Never argue with yourself about a truth heard for the first time; but mentally take it with you and, before going into The Silence, lay the puzzle before your Higher Self. You may not get immediate enlightenment, but sooner or later you will see that the matter has cleared up and apparently you have "thought it out" for yourself. You may get your answer most unexpectedly from a book, a letter, a lecture or a chance remark of a friend; but somehow you will get your answer. Finally you will gain the power of coming personally and CONSCIOUSLY into union with your Higher Self, who is one with God. You will then hear the spoken words that will answer every question. Do not expect this at first; but hunt for the answer and be ready to recognize it when given.

> "I have had many psychic experiences and am now sitting in a circle to develop into a spiritual medium. Will you please help me to become a medium?"

As to your experiences, you are evidently developing the ability to leave the physical body and come into contact with higher planes. And right here there is a great need for caution; for the denizens of the astral plane are of many sorts, just as there are entities upon the physical plane of many sorts. Unless you keep faithful watch over your "doors" some very undesirable visitors may enter your aura and your consciousness. To be what is known as a "medium" is far from desirable; for as the term is generally used it means one who allows himself to become negative and hands over his body to some discarnate entity to do with as it pleases. Remember, each person is held accountable and absolutely responsible both for his mentality and individuality. It makes no difference whether, through your negligence or ignorance, you vacate the premises and another enters who misuses your organism and faculties, YOU ARE STILL RESPONSIBLE. And if responsible, it is desirable that you remain in full command and able to open the "doors" to those whom you desire to enter and close them to all others. The lesson on NARCOTICS, ALCOHOL AND PSYCHICISM will give you the reasons.

Every gift unfolded, however, is yours to use. But as each one adds to your responsibility you must be careful to learn all about the laws governing such gifts that you may use them only for the glory of God. The only right way to contact the higher planes is to raise the vibrations of your physical body and its centers through a spiritual life, loving thoughts and helpful actions, until they vibrate in harmony with the key-note of the higher planes and at such a pitch that "no evil thing shall come nigh thy dwelling."

There are two ways to come into touch with the higher planes. The first is by vibrating to the spiritual note of love. To do this you must be clothed with spiritual atoms. You thus come into harmony with the spiritual plane and become aware of spiritual Beings whom you are temporarily able to contact because you vibrate in harmony with Them.

The second method is to make yourself negative and allow your physical vibrations to be so stilled that many physical atoms are easily loosened and detached and your vitality is drawn upon by ANY astral—NOT SPIRITUAL—entity who may wish to gather them and clothe himself in them and thus, temporarily, vibrate to the key-note of the physical plane and become temporarily recognizable on that plane.

In the first instance the whole experience will be uplifting and the spiritual atoms which you have contacted and drawn into your body will rejuvenate and strengthen it and will elevate your mind and advance you on the Path of Attainment. The second method will deplete and weaken your physical body, enervate your nervous system, dull your mentality and place a great stumbling block in your path if it does not lead to insanity or moral degeneration. This can easily be verified by following the history of the majority of subjective "mediums." They almost invariably end by becoming physical or moral wrecks and find it necessary to resort to stimulants; and the stimulants, by opening still wider the "doors" and weakening still more the control over the centers, but shortens the time ere the person is ruined.

The first method is a spiritually CONSTRUCTIVE process, the other a spiritually DESTRUCTIVE one. If you understand these facts and the fact that most entities upon the astral plane are not spiritual beings, but merely your friends with their dense and outer covering or garment (the physical body) removed, you will understand the danger of giving yourself up to their use.

You would hesitate to lend your body to any of your

friends on earth to do with as they pleased, and the mere passing over makes no difference whatever; they are able to use their astral faculties, which are a little finer than the physical; but that is all. They are just as spiritually advanced as when on earth; know just as much of the laws of life, but no more. Never give them any form of worship. Simply take such advice as they have to give as you would take their advice when upon earth, i.e. subject to your own good judgment and commonsense.

You can always be sure which of these two methods has been used by the effect on the psychics' physical body. If after the experience they are exhausted, tired, cross, fretful, nervous and uneasy, sometimes as long as a day or two, you can rest assured that they have allowed some entity to absorb their vital atoms and have allowed their physical vitality to clothe that entity according to the DESTRUCTIVE method. If, on the other hand, you find that their physical vitality is augmented; that a peaceful, happy and vigorous feeling remains, even for days after the experience; that life seems fuller, trials easier to bear and love more abundant, you can rest assured that they have risen above earthly things and have been clothed upon by the Spirit and have been enwrapped in spiritual atoms, and have descended into the astral only to cull its lessons for their own good and for the help of humanity.

You cannot always tell which of the above methods is being used from the teachings received at such a time; for in both cases the teachings may be helpful; but the fact remains that the first method is harmful to both the medium and to the entity who communicates. It is more a question of HOW the teachings are given than WHAT is given. No master of Wisdom, or anyone connected with The Great White Lodge, will ever give out teachings or even communicate, by the second and destructive method. No matter who the communicating entity may CLAIM to be, it will not be a Master of Wisdom.

The first or constructive method is the form of spiritual communion to be desired, not "mediumship." But do not strive even for this. Let it be a NATURAL GROWTH resulting from a life filled with loving thoughts and deeds.

> "I would like the House of the Interpreter to give me conclusive evidence that man is composed of different and independent entities called respectively: body, life, mind, soul, spirit. It has always been my opinion that these terms designate only different attributes of the organism." O. C.

You ask for "conclusive evidence," but you must bear in mind that, even in science, what is "conclusive" to one group of scientists is not to another. If by "conclusive evidence" you mean that you wish us to dissect the human body before your eyes and pull out life and mind and Soul as a nest of Chinese boxes might be pulled one from the other, we frankly admit that we cannot do it. If, however, you accept as conclusive the sort of evidence that science accepts in regard to imponderable things, we can give you conclusive evidence. For instance, no doubt you admit that you have a brain, altho you have never seen, weighed or measured it, nor can you find anyone who has ever seen, weighed or measured it. You may believe that you have a mind, but your own materialistic psychology says that you have nothing but automatic reactions to external and internal stimuli. Science says that you cannot PROVE that you exist, or that anything exists; that all things present themselves to your consciousness by their effect on your sense organs, the things themselves, possibly, being quite different from the report of them given by your senses. The evidence that man is a complex being made up of different entities must be judged by the manner in which your consciousness is affected, and hence can be conclusive only to yourself.

No materialistic "proof" can be given. There are those, however, who are willing to take the word of Those who have passed beyond the human stage and KNOW. This, of course, is not proof to you unless certain of your sense organs can respond to Their message.

We would not attempt to prove to you that "man is composed of different and independent entities"; for, as body, life, mind, Soul and Spirit manifest on the physical plane they are not wholly independent, but closely interrelated. When the life leaves the body you still have that you call "the human organism," but its so-called "attributes" have disappeared; the mind may depart and yet leave the organism and the life functioning apparently as well as before, as seen in idiots and the insane; the Soul and the Spirit may also be absent, yet the mind and the life may continue to function through the intact "human organism." If man were merely an automatic organism with "attributes," wherever you found the organism you would find the attributes. But, as we have seen above, any one or all of the attributes may be absent.

Our teaching is that the Soul is the immortal, reincarnating Ego, while the Spirit is the universal Breath of Divinity which animates the Soul or Ego just as the Breath of Life animates the physical body. The mind is a dual expression of the Soul, consisting of a Higher (spiritual) and a lower (brain) mind, the lower being but a reflection in physical matter of the Real Mind which is Spiritual Self-consciousness. Thus the REAL I is an immortal Soul having finite Spiritual Self-consciousness, overshadowed and animated by or filled with Infinite Spirit. This Real Self is spoken of as the Higher Self or the Father-in-heaven of the different religions, and manifest on earth through a vehicle composed of a physical body and its astral counterpart, and a reflection of the Spiritual Mind acting as Desire, all animated by Prana or life-force.

A good way to distinguish the Real Self is to eliminate everything that can be considered as a possession, i.e. my body, my mind, my life etc. You cannot say "my Spirit " any more than a sponge resting on the bed of the ocean can say "my water"; for it is said that, could the sponge last long enough, every drop of water in the ocean would pass through it, as well as through every other sponge. To say "my Spirit" is to limit Spirit which is Infinite. The Spirit moved upon the face of the waters in the beginning and must ever move in and through and over all creations. It is the Breath of Life of the Real Self. (Published in THE HOUSE OF THE INTERPRETER).

> "Tell me, brother, how best to cultivate and make strong the Spiritual Will." An Aspirant, Ohio.

You can strengthen your Spiritual Will by not trying. Just endeavor to interest yourself in spiritual matters, think pure thoughts and do kind deeds. Read books of an uplifting character. Study them not only with your head (intellect), but strive to enter into their deeper meaning with your heart (intuition). Know well that no matter how lofty a philosophy or how good a lesson, unless it brings to your individual Soul some practical application, something that you can work into your daily life, that philosophy or lesson is of no account to you. You cannot force yourself to will what you do not desire; but you can cultivate a desire for spirituality. And desire, being a lower note of the same octave, will of necessity awaken Will. (Published in THE HOUSE OF THE INTERPRETER).

"If a psychic receives a message given in the first person, i.e., if he is told to do certain things, perhaps a great work for humanity, and if with the message there comes a wonderful promise, I have been told that he only overheard a message given to humanity at large, and that only his poor, weak, human egotism makes him apply the message and the promise to himself. What is your teaching on this point?" Occult Student, Los Angeles, Cal.

The Elder Brothers of humanity, the great Masters of Wisdom, into whose hands the evolution of the Race is entrusted, are continually sending forth the cry for helpers. "The harvest truly is great, but the laborers are few;" for They can work on the earth plane only through human agencies. With the cry goes the promise of sure reward for all who hear and obey. The answer to your question is plainly given in Revelation XXII 17: "And the Spirit and the bride say, Come. And him that heareth say, Come. And let him that is athirst come. And whosoever will, let him take of the water of life freely."

None can hear unless their vibrations are keyed to the note of the call. When this takes place they hear the cry because it comes to them and enters their heart and understanding. What is everyone's business is seldom attended to; but he who hears, and understands his duty, to him does the message apply personally. Many reform movements appeal to the sympathy of all, but the Pharisees and Sadducees pass by on the other side. The one who hears the cry to help humanity and heeds it, even if he be only one of the humblest of the Samaritans, will stop and bind up the wounds of the helpless and accept the work as his own. To every one who thus hears, the promise is given. When the cry, "Come" is heard, instead of waiting for some one more worthy to answer first, the reply should be, "Here am I. Speak, Lord, for thy servant heareth."

If the Samaritan has done the work in a grandiose manner to be seen of men, or had he refused to allow anyone else to participate in that work for fear of losing the worldly honor for the deed, he would have been acting from "human egotism." And, no matter how faithfully he did the work, it would bring only bitterness and sorrow, and he could not claim the promised reward. He could not take of the water of life freely, because by the manner of doing the work he would prove that he had not yet overcome human egotism; and the promise is "unto him that overcometh."

When a psychic hears such a call let him or her at once determine to set about preparing himself or herself to obey the call in true humility and without false modesty, which is the outgrowth of egotism. (See lesson on MEMORY OF PAST LIVES.) (Published in THE HOUSE OF THE INTERPRETER).

PART X

MISCELLANEOUS

"Never utter these words: 'I do not know this—therefore it is false.' One must study to know, know to understand, understand to judge." Narada.

April 27th, 1908.
"I have regarded the human beings of today as the descendants of a species of human animals, if one may call them so. . . . Am I correct?"

Your query as to the descent of man from an human animal can only be touched upon here. For fuller information on this point we refer you to THE SECRET DOCTRINE, Vol. I, where you will find all about the different stages of man and about the apes etc. If you do not have access to the unabridged work in your public library, we would advise you to get the abridged edition.

The subject is too long for a letter, but, briefly stated, man descended from the gods who breathed into evolved animal forms the Divine Breath of Life (GENESIS II-7), that through these animal bodies he might gain experience on the lowest or earth plane. The task given to each Soul therefore, is to redeem the physical atoms with which it clothes itself and, through the experience thus gained, evolve back to the starting point plus the experience and knowledge gained. Redemption means the redemption of all the atoms of all the various bodies that the Fathers (Pitris—the "gods" or the Fathers-in-heaven) have given in your keeping. By redeeming your own body that much of the earth is uplifted and spiritualized. And that is the only way the earth can be redeemed; for, every vibration of spiritual force to which the human monad responds, sends an answering wave of force through the whole cosmos. Thus, by man and through man, shall the earth be redeemed.

Therefore you are quite right in saying that circumstances neither make nor mar the spiritual growth of man. For the moment he identifies himself, even imperfectly, with his Father-in-heaven—his very personal and individual god—he becomes master of his conditions, ruler over circumstance and Savior of his bodies and his animal nature—in a word, is Lord of his Kingdom. Then he literally sits down at the right hand of his Father, and his enemies (his desires and animal appetites) are his foot-stool and are the servants of his will.

Reincarnation is the only logical unravelling of the mystery of life, and a person is blind and wandering in the dark until he finds this lifeline. Then at once all begins to shape itself, and in the fulness of time all the crooked places are made straight and life unfolds like the pages of a beautiful book. We never mind bearing trials when we know that they are merely correcting mistakes made in a past life, or else learning needed lessons in this. Trials are not given as punishments; but as the only means of making us learn the lessons that will fit us to take our real places at the right hand of God-the-Father, and to gain a greater realization of His nearness and help while here below. You have the correct attitude of waiting for more light instead of denouncing what, for the time, is beyond your comprehension.

June 17th, 1908.

"I was delighted with some of the teachings of. . . . and was therefore very glad that I was going to meet her personally. But no sooner did I lay my eyes upon her and hear her speak, than I felt sorely disappointed. . . . Finally she repelled me to such an extent that I actually felt aversion to her. . . . Her lectures about. . . . appear to me simply ridiculous, it simply seems absurd, nay, childish nonsense. Some of the articles in the. . . . for June, especially one by Mr. . . . seem to me ridiculous and rather sad. Owing to these circumstances I am sometimes beset with doubts as to the truthfulness of the. . . . teachings."

There is a strong tendency on your part, which it will be well for you to look in the face and recognize for what it is, to judge with human judgment the acts and teachings of others. The Christ, through Jesus, the man, said: "Judge not that ye be not judged. For with what judgment ye judge, ye shall be judged;" meaning that if you bring your sister or brother up before the judgment-seat of the wisdom of the mere worldly conception of what is "nonsense, ridiculous," etc., you yourself must be content with and must expect to be judged from no higher standpoint. You must make your life, your physical appearance and your words conform absolutely to the outer letter of the law—failure must mean condemnation to you. Try to realize that you have nothing to do with the failure or success of anyone but your own personality, and that one lesson alone stands out plainly and distinctly so that "He who runs may read" i.e. "Be ye not conformed to this world, but be ye transformed by the renewal of your minds." This means that we must renew our minds by changing our ways of thinking. Instead of looking for the mote in the eye of your sister or brother, seek diligently for the beam that is in your own eye.

You will never find Truth in any teachings if Truth, to you, depends upon the perfection of the instrument through which that Truth is expressed. Truth confronts you on every side. Therefore, dear brother, learn to seek Truth for Truth's sake. Look for it among the stubble and muck of life and in the dark places where humanity crawls in filth; look for it hidden under the mountains of selfishness and self-sufficiency of teachers; seek for it as a Jewel of Great Price that has been lost; for you may find the Jewel where you least expect it. But first rise up and sweep your own house diligently.

No Master, or even a Savior, can dispel your doubts; for they are the natural result of your attitude. Until you learn the lesson of separating Truth from personality your doubts will never be set at rest. Consider carefully the saying found in I Cor. II 14: "But the natural receiveth not the things of the Spirit of God: for they are foolishness unto him: neither can he know them, because they are spiritually discerned." All this means, dear brother, that you must cultivate the power of spiritual discernment and not allow anything to turn you aside from Truth. Truth often comes in most repulsive disguises, and it is a test to the Soul to recognize it and separate the grain from the husks, not swallowing them to get the grain. You might as well swallow a walnut whole because the kernel is sweet and wholesome. Do as you would with any material thing presented to you: crack the nut, no matter how black and repellant the shell, and extract the Kernel.

April 2nd, 1908.

"Where does imagination spring from? Does it entirely belong to the subconscious, or to a sort of central point between the soul and the subconscious? Why does it attack me and carry me away into the future tense, offering pessimism? Is the reason why it affects me so strongly due to my being under a deep earthy sign? it belonging to the moon?"

Imagination is a function of the Soul. It is the power derived from the Higher Self for the purpose, through deliberately willing it, of creating upon the mental plane. Pessimism has nothing in common with it, nor does the subconscious control it. But happy is the man who has the subconscious under the control of the imagination; for it is by this power that the true image of the Real Self is created, and by it is the link between the personality and the individuality made strong.

Beware of confusing imagination with fancy or idle dreaming. Fancy is born of the rhythm of the vibrations of the subconscious, and is either pessimistic, fearful or egotistical or any other thing which, by being long indulged in, has been able to set up a vibratory center in the subconscious. Such a center will continue to vibrate in the same key until the Higher Will comes in and, through the power of imagination, changes the rate of its vibration. The sign of your nativity cannot affect this power; but the tendency to pessimism is no doubt strengthened by the planetary influence. Do not get confused—it is fancy that tends to pessimism. By proper use of imagination you must impart a new vibration to the subconscious. Determine to create new images of happiness and success; and with all the power of Will, MAKE the subconscious respond. Never give in to the old vibrations. This is one of the most important lessons for you to learn in this incarnation.

April 20th, 1908.

"Without being impatient for advanced work or intellectual diversions I should be greatly interested to learn the occult significance and place of music and geometry. 'God geometrizes' has always been a dark saying to me,—the only sense in which I can comprehend it being that certain numbers play an important part in the manifested universe, like 3 in the fundamental constituents of the universe, and in the modes of intellect, the dimensions of space, etc. Or like the number 7 in the tones of the octave, or in the colors of the spectrum, etc."

You have a correct idea of the saying, "God geometrizes", and study along that line will open vistas of unexpected interest. Take geometry to include not only form but number, color and sound as well. This makes the square the symbol of all manifestation that pertains to earth. Man is composed of seven principles, four lower—the square—and three higher—the triangle. (See THE SECRET DOCTRINE, Vol. II, p 625 et seq.) Study the formation of crystals, even snow or frost crystals, and you will at once see the geometrical forms that vapor takes upon crystallizing. Also look up the common experiment in physics of covering a metal plate with fine sand and then vibrating the plate with a bow, and note how every different note or tone produces a characteristic geometrical figure in the sand on the plate. All forces (vibrations) when expressing in (i.e. condensed into) matter act along geometrical lines. The designs produced are not haphazard formations but are the mathematical expressions of certain thoughtforms (vibrations) from the higher planes. Every material form, from crystal to man, is the mathematical, and indeed the only possible, expression of certain combinations of vibrations (ideas) upon the higher planes, the universe as a whole being an expressed thought-form of the Absolute. Thoughts, being forces, must express along geometrical lines that are mathematically exact.

A deep study of plant life will convince you that the form, number and color of every leaf and flower expresses itself also in sound and, were your ears attuned to Nature's voice, you would find each perfect flower a symphony expressing the characteristics of the particular plant to which it belonged. Moreover, for those who can read, Nature is an open book and there are "Tongues in trees, books in running brooks, sermons in stones"; for the form, color and number of everything that grows tells man the inner meaning of the plant together with its uses for man. For those who study her Nature speaks with no uncertain voice. "Who hath ears to hear let him hear."

June 21st, 1908.

"I will say that by studying the papers you have sent me I find myself comprehending truths that I did not realize before. I find myself getting nearer, and realize enough to feel confidence in the teachings given and to have no doubts as to their source. They attract me as a magnet, and are drawing me nearer all the while. In connection with this I wish to ask if it is right and proper to look forward to, and bend my efforts in that direction, and try to attain to, the conditions that will make an immediate return possible after passing out of this body?"

We are happy to hear that your brain consciousness is registering the nearness of your Teachers; for it is a living reality. But, until you could sense it, it would be mere words to you. If you were stone blind and deaf, you might be in the midst of ravishing beauty and close to strains of heavenly music; but until your eyes were opened and your ears unstopped you could not well perceive the beauty and harmony that surrounded you.

As to your question about immediate reincarnation, that is a matter which is under your own control if there is a reason great enough to make the sacrifice necessary. It may be that your Higher Self is impressing upon you the fact that such a return will take place, as a warning to you to make every preparation. Remember that there is always a Karma that must, of necessity, be worked out on the physical plane; but as the time of ex-carnation is a time of assimilation and growth—a time for digesting the experience gained—the preparation for the loss of this period by immediate reincarnation should be a careful assimilation while here. That is, make a great effort to go slow and digest and assimilate all experiences. Learn to seek in every event its inner meaning and bearing on life. Seek its why and wherefore. Try to chew slowly and digest as you go along. The danger in an immediate reincarnation (which is by no means as rare as some suppose) is that the astral body does not have time to separate from the body of desire, and, being full of vigor, it attaches itself to the newly formed astral body and becomes a "Dweller on the Threshold" much more tangible, that is more dense and earthly, than the ordinary "Dweller" which all must face. In such exceptional cases this dense "Dweller" is so close to the reincarnating Ego that it becomes a haunting presence throughout life, and any old, unconnected faults and tendencies of the past are apt to be intensified rather than corrected in the new incarnation. Unless all this is understood in a practical way and prepared for, very little advance can be made in such an incarnation, the two life-periods becoming like one physical expression without time for rest and assimilation between. It would be much like eating your breakfast and immediately eating your dinner to save time at noon.

There is a way, however, FOR THOSE WHO KNOW—a way which the wise and determined can find—that will prolong one life-period over the period usually occupied by two or more, if there is work of such importance that it demands continued presence on the physical plane. Eugene Sue's fictitious tale of THE WANDERING JEW, and many other tales of similar character, is founded upon a physiological and psychological possibility that has been demonstrated more than once. But it is well to consider the suffering and loneliness entailed, unless you have gained Wisdom and Mastery ere experimenting. It might be of advantage to your spiritual growth IF the effort made you more diligent and better prepared to gain such mastery over the desire-body while in the flesh as to leave it with very little strength to haunt a new life, or to gain Mastery NOW so that even passing out would be unnecessary. As you say, you are no coward and no drone. Therefore, we say, if you are strongly impressed to take this path, go forward in the power and might of the Spirit. DARE-DO-KEEP SILENT.

June 22nd, 1908.

"I cannot report much progress, I am disgusted with myself. . . . I have sold hares to. . . . medical school! And pets at that!! I always keep them on my place for eating, but to sell them TO BE TORTURED! for a very little money! I simply feel degraded in my own eyes. And you see I am almost a hopeless case, for anyone who would do that surely is not fit for the Kingdom. They tell me they are etherized but I do not believe it, as that would defeat their own ends. They tell me it is for 'the benefit of science,' but that is not what I sell them for!"

We have received your letter of self-depreciation and we must tell you, dear sister, that self-depreciation, without a determined effort to overcome the faults you depreciate, will soon degenerate into morbid self-pity rather than self-respect and proper assertiveness. When you know a thing is wrong never give yourself a chance to make an excuse, but hold the whip-hand and keep the reins steady until the obstreperous self goes along the path marked out.

The Master Jesus said: "It must be that these things come into the world, but woe unto him by whom they come," and this is true of all suffering. The poor animals which suffer that humanity may be benefited are not given a chance to make the suffering a vicarious atonement altho the suffering pushes them forward in their evolution. Yet, since it is forced upon them and, from their point of view, is the result of cruelty, it leaves its imprint upon the matter of their subconsciousness. As this matter is taken up again and again until it is finally redeemed at the end of its evolution by coming under the selfconscious dominion of an human Ego, this cruelty will manifest after its kind all along the path of evolution. No matter what sort of a body such atoms may be incorporated in, the sense of cruelty and suffering unjustly caused will endeavor to work out in an effort to adjust the balance, and will prey upon humanity in some way and give back suffering for suffering. This is one of the chief ways in which the law of Karma works. There must be an adjustment. If the pendulum swings too violently to the left it must swing correspondingly to the right until from the very force of extremes, a balance is attained. It makes little difference as far as the Law of Retribution works out, if the doctors do think they are justified and that a corresponding good will result to the human race. There is but one law, namely, all things reproduce after their kind.

There are always two effects to every cause or impulse set up; the out-going vibration of the initial impulse and the return wave which comes back to the point of departure. You can easily prove this by casting a small stone into a still, smooth pond; for there is but one Law of Vibration. The vibrations (ripples) will go out from the point where the stone was cast in ever widening circles; but when they reach the boundary of the pond they will return to the exact spot from which they started. This is an illustration of the absolute and IMPERSONAL action of the Law of Karma. Through the suffering of the animals the doctors may find certain apparently successful ways of helping humanity; but the return wave will bring to humanity more widespread suffering, cruelty and inhumanity, and will react especially upon those who had anything, either directly or indirectly, to do with the initial cruelty. In the epidemics of disease that sweep over the country some escape, some recover and some succumb; but all must bear the Karma of the diseased conditions in the earth's aura: it is the world's Karma. The ones who succumb are the ones who have brought to themselves a personal Karma by being instrumental in sowing, in past lives, conditions that result in disease; those who escape probably did nothing toward creating such conditions. Some have the disease in a mild form and some have it severely; but all in exact proportion to the sowing. "Whatsoever a man soweth, that shall he also reap." The harvest may not ripen for ages; but it will be exact and just when it comes.

Animals, altho drugged motionless, suffer far more than human beings under the same conditions, because an human being when under an anesthetic at once leaves the earth plane and, necessarily, the suffering, and, unless exceedingly earthly, is taken care of on the higher planes, often receiving most wonderful lessons and experiencing the greatest happiness. But the poor animal, not having a Higher Self and working out its evolution entirely on the physical and lower astral planes, has nothing to compensate it for the cruel loss of its birthright, i.e. a normal, healthy existence on the earth plane. Hence its whole evolution is retarded. As the animal can go no higher, the anesthetic merely removes its consciousness from the physical to the lower astral — the astral body as you know being the seat of sensation — where it is fully conscious of all that is going on and where it experiences all the suffering altho unable to express it through its paralyzed body. The doctors are no doubt sincere in thinking that the anesthetized animals do not suffer; but it is only because they are ignorant of what is taking place upon the astral plane.

July 13th, 1908.
"Your kind letter concerning hares was read eagerly. Am following your advice and have tonight written the. . . . laboratory that I cannot supply them any more. My husband takes it easier than I thought he would. I am very much happier. Thank you many, many times for telling me the TRUTH."

"I am not at all conversant with Theosophy, and am puzzled by the reference to 'the incoming Sixth Sub-race.' Perhaps you will kindly explain."

The subject is too vast to be more than hinted at in this column, but, briefly, the Secret Doctrine teaches that the humanity of this globe manifests in seven Great Races called Root-Races. Each Root-Race is composed of seven successive sub-races, and the sub-races of nations, tribes, etc. All white and red peoples belong to the Aryan or Fifth Root-Race, and most of the Western peoples belong to the fifth sub-race of the Aryan. The yellow races of the East are the remnants of the last sub-races of the Atlantean or Fourth Root-Race which perished as a Race with the sinking of the continent of Atlantis. The sixth sub-race of the Aryan will evolve upon the American continent, and even now has begun. (See lesson on THE SIXTH ANGEL.) (This letter was published in "The House of the Interpreter.")

March 3rd, 1908.
"If people choose their next environment why do they dislike it so?. . . . What can one do to prevent having to come back again?"

The Soul does not choose incarnation from the standpoint of what will give the most pleasure, but from the standpoint of what environment will give the Soul the best discipline and which will best teach it the lessons most needed to bring it into at-one-ment with the Father-in-heaven. Generally the discipline the Soul most needs is that which is irksome to the personality, and it is difficult for the Soul to make the personality understand that the incarnation is for the purpose of overcoming some particular trait and conquering the conditions in which it was made.

The only way to prevent coming back again is to learn

all the lessons, gain all the experience of the earth life, so that when the Soul has completed its earthly evolution there is nothing left for it to experience. Even then one would have to be very sure that, having gained all experience, he had also stilled all compassion for humanity so that he would not be tempted to come back to help those who were still struggling with sin and ignorance.

April 14th
"In your lesson on Purity you say, 'The lower animals having no spark of the Divine dwelling within them,' etc. As I hold that they are in every way as Divine as myself, I am somewhat in a quandary."

The exception you take to our statement that "the lower animals having no spark of the Divine dwelling in them" can be readily understood by a knowledge of the Law. While this subject is too great to be properly treated in a letter we will try to give you an outline, altho some of the statements are more in the nature of hints and without further explanation are bound to be more or less misleading.

In brief, the Spark of Divinity or the reincarnating Ego clothes itself in atoms belonging to each kingdom successively, mineral, vegetable and animal. It is always the same Divine Spark, but when manifesting in the lower kingdoms it is so disseminated through them that it is not individualized in any one expression; for no one vehicle is capable of expressing it. In passing through the degrees of the animal kingdom from the lowest forms to the highest, say from an earth worm (you could, of course, go much lower) to a horse or dog, its manifestation gradually condenses or tends to become individualized. That is, while the One Life animates the earth worm it takes a great mass of such worms to express even rudimentary animal consciousness, and no one worm can be said to have even an animal soul. The lower animal kingdom is animated by an animal soul, of course, but it would take about all the earth worms there are to express an animal soul.

As animal life advances in the scale the animal soul expresses itself more and more completely, because it has better instruments for its use and thus requires fewer individuals to express it. Thus the functions and attributes of the animal soul are expressed in an ascending scale until instinct is reached. When instinct in its fullness is expressed— instinct being the highest vibration the animal soul is capable of expressing—the Divine Spark begins to overshadow the animal. In this way instinct gradually melts into and is overlapped by intelligence and reason which, in turn, reach their highest note in intuition. Animals which function in the higher animal kingdoms have the animal soul expressed in its fullness and in addition have the overshadowing of the Divine Spark. This overshadowing, however, is not individualized, many animals being overshadowed by the one Ego. For this reason they may, and often do, exhibit traits that make them more lovable than many human beings. This is because they are perfect animals, overshadowed and willingly led and guided by a Divine Ego, still they have not as yet been given the portion of goods that will come to them from their Father. In short animals are our younger brothers. They are in the kindergarten of life, acting in accordance with the overshadowing Law of Evolution without free-will to disobey. If they develop vicious traits, as some few do, still they are not responsible, for such traits are imparted to or taught them by man through cruel treatment or through man's evil thought emanations. Of themselves they cannot sin, for they are but following the Law of Evolution and, like the flowers, are expressing the fullness of their being.

At the time of death the overshadowing Ego gathers together all the animal atoms composing all the individuals that came under its particular ray and builds a more perfect animal structure which will possess, as inherent faculties, all the experience which it has gained in previous animal lives. This has been demonstrated by the experiments of certain scientific botanists who have found that new species do not develop or evolve gradually from already existing types, but spring into being suddenly and without warning in one generation.

This assimilation and advanced expression goes on until the Ego has built up an organism capable of expressing the Divine, i.e. is made in the image of God and capable of containing a Spark of the Divine—the Human. At this point the guiding reins are given into the hands of the animal-man. He now has free-will and a mind capable of reasoning and thinking as an individual. He can choose to walk in the light, guided by his Father-in-heaven, or he can refuse and pay the penalty. The choice is his and he is also responsible for his choice. He has become a creator and from hence forth he is Lord over the lower kingdoms; by his thoughts he can lift them up or debase them. Because of this power and the fact that ALL EVIL IS THE RESULT OF MAN'S DISOBEDIENCE—not disobedience to the commands of any higher Being, but to The Law he must suffer from evil conditions until he has learned consciously to follow and obey The Law of his being just as, while an animal, he obeyed it blindly and instinctively. But it is well to remember that there are no sudden jumps from one kingdom to another. The individualization of the animal-man takes place gradually; many of the lower types of savages having not yet reached complete individualization—they are more individualized than the higher animals, but are not entirely personalized. Since the animals take their savagery from man, when he is just entering the human kingdom animal-man must express that savagery in human form and work through it to higher things.

As to the immortality of animals, nothing that lives can die. The higher animal, such as the horse, dog and elephant, is gradually merged into a human animal (does not BECOME one). All perfected consciousness, with its overshadowing Divinity, must go on evolving until a better vehicle of expression is obtained. All life is immortal, but conscious immortality can only be obtained by merging the human into the Divine as the animal is merged into the human. As man is animal, but more than animal, so is the Divine man, but more than man. A good illustration of this law of individualization is found in the rose. In its wild state a rose has but a single row of petals, five in number. It grows and blossoms in great profusion, often covering a whole hill-side, yet, while the whole mass will perfume the air all around, a single rose, when plucked, will seemingly be devoid of perfume and have little beauty, its few petals dropping almost immediately. As the rose is cultivated, however, it gains more petals, gives out more perfume and requires fewer bushes to grow on until, in the American Beauty rose, the perfection of its culture is reached, it requiring a whole bush to produce one perfect flower. But this one flower can give out as much perfume as the whole hillside of wild roses gave out. It has as many petals, all securely fastened together, and will last many times longer than its wild sister after being plucked. In short, it has evolved the Soul of the Rose—the Rose being the highest type of flower. You will find this law illustrated in all Nature, from grass, which grows in many blades, up to the oak. Also from the baser minerals up to gold.

Understanding this Law of Evolution you can learn many lessons from the animals, especially those of love, fidelity, faithfulness and forgiveness of injury and ill-treatment. Bear in mind that they are doing instinctively what man must learn to do consciously and of his own free-will. They are really examples for man to follow; for Nature has already worked out and placed before his eyes every problem that confronts him.

A horse or dog may have many incarnations as a horse or dog so you may have been associated with them as horses or dogs in past lives. This is frequently illustrated by a dog suddenly seeing a man and persistently following him thereafter; he has simply recognized a former master and refuses to be driven away by the fact that the recognition is not mutual. A look into the speaking eyes of such a dog will convince you that he really does recognize you and cannot understand why you fail to give him the accustomed welcome. The sorrow expressed is most pathetic if you persist in driving such a dog away.

One more point. It is possible for such animals to be overshadowed by the same Divine Spark that overshadows you, and in such cases you will never lose your animal companions, for when they are more than animal you will be more than man.

Your difficulty arises from the fact that what you refer to as the Divine Spark is in reality but Divine Essence or Divine Creative Force evolving through the kingdoms. The Divine Spark is this force not universally disseminated throughout the universe, but personalized.

June 1st, 1908.

"Why is it that in the Teachings of THE ORDER OF THE 15 we hear nothing about 'loyalty to leaders' when that is such a prominent feature of many occult societies? Is it not true that loyalty to leaders is the first and most important duty of the Neophyte?"

You are quite right in your idea that loyalty is the first step and, we might say, the most important TO YOUR OWN SOUL were there any degrees of importance when every step must be faithfully taken.

Loyalty, however, must not be a blind following, but must be tempered with Wisdom and must be the result of an intuitive understanding of the guidance given by the Higher

Self. Many a leader has passed out of the physical body leaving his or her work to be wrecked in the quicksands of mistaken zeal by a misunderstanding of this law.

A leader is one who goes ahead. Necessarily such an one is subjected to dangers and pitfalls which those who follow may have the power to see. We think a little thought will convince you that loyalty demands that the followers, at least the more intuitional, must guard the leader by watching out for ambushed enemies and warn the leader of danger when signs of ambition, selfishness, self-righteousness, or any compromise with truth or purity begin to show themselves. And thus, by the power of their developed intuition and by their true love and sympathy, prove a body-guard in the real sense of the word, while the main body of followers should have the personality of the leader thrust upon them as little as possible.

Followers should be faithful and loyal to the teachings rather than to the personality of the leader; for the Great Law will take care of all, and no matter how much loyalty is demanded by a leader, he or she will receive just as much as he or she deserves. The Law says, "Give and it shall be given unto you," and this will be in exact justice, not only in what measure, but also in what kind. If a leader gives his or her followers love, sympathy and devotion, forgetting self and striving only to lead the way and make straight the Path for those who follow, he or she will receive back again from the main body of followers true loyalty and love, and the few who repay with selfishness and criticism the love-force will drop from the ranks with scarcely a ripple.

APPENDIX

MORNING PRAYER

I have within me the power of The Christ.
I can conquer all that comes to me today.
I am strong enough to bear every trial and
   accept every joy, and say,
"Thy will be done."

PRAYER OF CONSECRATION

We, recognizing the omnipotent power of the Great Creative Force, do make most solemn covenant to present our whole selves, our bodies, our minds, our Souls, a living sacrifice to Thee.

We yield all personal desires unto the one Great Desire, to be used as instruments to create a center through which The Lodge can work.

Recognizing the oneness of Thine All-pervading Force, we give back to Thee, for Thy use, all that we possess, and by the power of The Living Christ, demand that all obstacles be removed, and Thy work be speedily established in perfect justice.

HEALING PRAYER

O thou loving and helpful Master Jesus! Thou who gavest to Thy disciples power to heal the sick!

We, recognizing Thee, and realizing Thy divine presence with us, ask Thee to lay Thy hands upon us in healing love.

Cleanse us from all our sins, and by the divine power of Omnipotent Life, drive out the atoms of inharmony and disease, and fill our bodies full to overflowing with Life, and Love, and Purity.

ANNOUNCEMENT

"BEHOLD, I BRING UNTO YOU GOOD TIDINGS OF GREAT JOY."

To all students of the higher life who truly desire to progress, and who wish the opportunity of coming into closer personal touch with those Masters of Wisdom who through all ages have been the Teachers, Guides and Elder Brothers of humanity, there comes the following message:

In accordance with the geometrical design of the universe, a point is now reached when an advanced Order from the Great White Lodge can be established upon the earth plane. This Order is not an organization in the general acceptation of the term, NOR IS IT CONNECTED EITHER WITH THE OUTER OR INNER WORK OF ANY OCCULT ORGANIZATION NOW IN EXISTENCE ON THE PHYSICAL PLANE. IT IS A NEW AND DIRECT OUTPUT FROM THE GREAT WHITE LODGE. According to its fundamental principles, only such earnest students can be admitted to it as have proven their devotion to the Masters, and have sent out their cry to Them for enlightenment and help. All such persons are welcomed into this Order, and such probationary lessons will be sent them, from time to time, as will afford them an opportunity of coming into close fellowship and conscious communication with the Masters of Wisdom. Understand this point clearly. It will be ONLY THROUGH YOUR OWN INDIVIDUAL EFFORT, your attitude of soul, and the character of your life that will enable YOU TO PLACE YOURSELF in personal, conscious touch with the Masters. IT DEPENDS UPON NO PERSONALITY BUT YOUR OWN.

No vows, or pledges, are asked of you, for only those are eligible to this Order who have voluntarily given up their lives to the higher law, and have already vowed allegiance to their own Higher Self. Therefore, this Order offers the opportunity of fulfilling past vows and no new ones are required. Membership in this Order will not conflict with any duties of life, or with membership in other organizations, or membership in any religious denomination.

In such an Order dues, as such, would be impossible, but as the lessons must be printed and mailed, it is expected that all who desire the help will voluntarily aid the work by contributions in accordance with their ability and the law of exact justice. It is a primal law of occultism that, no matter how much is set before you, you are able to assimilate (get) in exact ratio with the spirit of helping others that you display. "Give and it shall be given unto you; good measure, pressed down and shaken together, and running over—for with the same measure that ye mete withal, it shall be measured to you again." Only by such co-operation can the work be carried on.

If you are interested in this matter and would like to hear further concerning it, we would be glad to have you address the Secretary, who will refer your letter for reply, and forward the same to you as soon as received. In your letter we would be pleased to have you tell something of your spiritual life, and your desires as to further study, together with a brief description of any remarkable visions, dreams or psychic experiences that you may have had recently.

Address replies to

P. O. Box 607,   F. HOMER CURTISS, M. D.,
Denver, Colo., U. S. A.

CIRCULAR OF INFORMATION

In response to many requests for information concerning this new Order, we announce that it is a continuation of the work started by the Masters of the Great White Lodge, through Madame Blavatsky, in 1875, under the name of the Theosophical Society. But as no organization can contain the wisdom of The Lodge that Society was but a phase of the work, and a means of propagating the seed that has now been sown broadcast over the world. Many students have outgrown organizations, having found them too narrow and their necessary limitations too binding. This is but a natural feature of growth and again proves the great law "As above, so below;" just as the seed, when first planted, is confined in a protective sheath from which, in the process of growth, it will burst forth.

One of the chief objects of this Movement is to correlate advanced theosophical teachings with the orthodox Christian teachings; to form a neutral ground where both can meet and recognize Truth. On this account we may disappoint many intellectual theosophists, for our language will purposely be made simple, and the great truths which we set forth will be so stated as to appeal to minds schooled in Western religious thought. Our great object is to enable all sections of spiritual seekers, New Thought, Spiritualism, Theosophy, Christianity, in fact all lovers of Truth, to draw together at the heart centre. THIS IS A NECESSARY PREPARATION FOR THE NEAR ADVENT OF THE AVATAR; for the good news of His quick coming must be given "unto all people," not to a few intellectual thinkers. All schools of spiritual thought need this preparation.

In this present age the Masters must work through human agencies, and the moment that you determine to give of yourself and your worldly substance, you become a recognized agent of The Lodge. All organizations and movements which receive help from The Lodge, have their own particular work to do. Whether they have succeeded in the task set before them, or whether they have failed, is clearly shown by their results. They all receive help in exact proportion to the degree that they accomplish their task and make themselves pure channels through which the force can be poured. We criticise no one, and we make no all-inclusive claims. Results alone will show who are back of us.

As we explain in our first lesson this is an Order into which certain Souls will be drawn, but not necessarily all who ask for help, although all will be helped to grow toward that point. When admission into the Order occurs there will be an outward recognition, and obligations, but no obligations, except the privacy of papers, are required before that time.

To each one who expresses a desire to become one of us we plan to send a lesson each month. These lessons will be private, and in many cases personal, therefore we will request that, when marked "private," they be not revealed to others. All papers will be private, but those not specially marked "private" may be shown to interested friends at your discretion. They are not, however, to be shown promiscuously or left lying around to be seen by everyone.

A SIMPLE ANNOUNCEMENT OF YOUR DESIRE TO STUDY WITH US and a realization of your obligation to help us in return is all that is necessary. The help we ask is just what your conscience tells you is the right and proper thing to do in accordance with your worldly means. Many will be unable to give financial aid and from those we ask love and helpful thoughts. If we DEMANDED financial aid we would at once put ourselves outside the radius of The Lodge force, therefore we simply trust and believe that the means to print and distribute these lessons, and carry on the work, will be forthcoming. All who hear the call in their hearts will be ready and willing to help. In this connection we may state that there are no persons to be supported and no salaries to officers to be paid out of the funds.

All contributions, both large and small, will be gratefully received and promptly acknowledged. The ones who give ten cents because they love the Master's work may bring to themselves a greater blessing than those who might give dollars without any thought or sacrifice. No matter what amount given, the real offering is the loving desire to help. "Let every man do according as he is disposed in his heart, not grudgingly, or of necessity, for God loveth a cheerful giver."

PLEASE STUDY THIS CIRCULAR CAREFULLY, AS IT WILL SAVE YOU ASKING MANY USELESS QUESTIONS ABOUT MATTERS ALREADY DISTINCTLY STATED. YOU WILL THUS SAVE US MUCH VALUABLE TIME AND UNNECESSARY CORRESPONDENCE.

ORGANIZATIONS

Altho we emphasized our relation to organizations in our first circular by placing the statement in italics, yet it seems to have been overlooked by many. Therefore we will restate our position more fully herewith, so that in the future there may be no question as to the significance of this Movement and its relation to all others.

This Movement is not an organization because it has no constitution or by-laws, no officers (except the Secretary), requires no pledges and no dues, and does not restrict a member's activity in any society or organization. Therefore it is not antagonistic to any existing organization that is helping humanity, but permits perfect freedom. All that is necessary for membership is to express a sincere desire for help in your efforts for spiritual growth.

Since the treatment accorded to all former agents selected by The Lodge has proved conclusively that humanity is not yet ready to be entrusted with the knowledge of the personalities of the agents through whom these teachings are given, it has been considered best that, on this occasion, they remain incognito; for the agents are of no more importance, from the standpoint of the work, than would be a pipe through which a stream of pure water is conveyed into a parched and thirsty land. Those who are athirst for the Living Waters will drink from the stream, those who are not will pass it by.

AS TO OTHER MOVEMENTS

We can but reiterate that while WE ARE NOT CONNECTED, IN ANY WAY, WITH THE OUTER AND INNER WORK OF ANY ORGANIZATION NOW ON THE EARTH PLANE, nevertheless we stand for Truth wherever found, our motto being, "By their fruits ye shall know them."

Under no circumstance do we criticize any. If an organization, society or movement has helped one Soul to take one step upon The Path to Mastery it has not wrought in vain. The fact that a teaching attracts and helps you is evidence that it contains the lesson needed by you for the step you are taking. The fact that a movement no longer appeals to you, no matter how helpful it may be to others, is evidence either that your Soul has learned the lessons that movement had for you—even though not mastered intellectually or that the movement, no matter how beautifully conceived and launched, has become tainted with something that is not helpful, or perhaps is distinctly injurious, to your physical, mental, moral or spiritual growth. . . .

Each movement that aims to help humanity has its own place and its own work. Colored blocks are necessary in the kindergarten, primers for children, text-books for the training of the mind in school and college; but when the mind has been trained it must then put that training to use in a practical way; in business, under the head

Our correspondence is so large that we cannot answer letters immediately, but will always endeavor to do so within one week after their receipt of the firm or manager; in art, under a great teacher; in spiritual things, under a Master of Wisdom. But remember that, because you are no longer interested in the colored blocks or primers you once thought so beautiful, you are not to despise the children who still cling to them, or find fault with the teachers of the a b c's. All have their place, and the children will grow away from the blocks when they have learned their lessons just as you have grown. Every uplifting movement or teaching has its place and has for followers those who need its lessons. The Master Jesus said, "Whosoever shall give to drink unto one of these little ones a cup of cold water only in the name of a disciple, verily I say unto you, he shall in no wise lose his reward!   *   *   *   Inasmuch as ye have done it unto one of the least of these, my brethren, ye have done it unto me."

AIMS OF THIS MOVEMENT

The great wave of psychicism now sweeping over the land has brought many students to the point where their inner faculties are unfolding. This is a point of great danger, for here the two paths—the Right Hand and the Left Hand—diverge. This Order may be called a wayside House of Rest, placed at the point of divergence of the paths, at whose door every pilgrim who knocks finds welcome, and within rest, sympathy, understanding and encouragement, and also a guide to lead him safely past the many dangers and pitfalls that surround the entrance to the Right Hand Path. This is a personal work which cannot be accomplished by any organization bound by set rules.

Although the Christian Bible is the greatest occult book ever given to humanity—for it contains not only the wisdom of all prior scriptures, but also a prophecy of the future, yet it is the least understood of any scripture, because heretofore all efforts to explain it have been upon a literal, intellectual, material and historical basis and not from the standpoint of its spiritual symbology and esoteric meaning. The Christian religion is universally acknowledged to be the greatest factor in modern civilization, and the time has come for it to take an advanced step through an understanding of the esoteric meaning of its sacred mysteries,[1] and by a relization that its teachings symbolize the same vital truths common to all religions, thus taking the first step on the return journey to the one Wisdom Religion.

As all religions, sects and creeds contain at least a germ of Truth, our aim is to help each one to find that germ IN THEIR OWN TEACHINGS, and purify and develop it into the Tree of Life in their own garden.

The Christian missionaries are censured by many for forcing what, to their minds, is a superior form of truth, upon people who already have a religion, the inner teachings of which the missionaries have not the faintest idea. At the same time, those who are

---

[1] Jesus said to his initiated disciples: "Unto you it is given to know the mystery of the kingdom of God, but unto them that are without (i.e., not initiated) all these things are done in parables."—Mark IV, 11.

thus criticizing the missionaries are, in their turn, insisting that all Christian people shall accept certain spiritual teachings couched in terms that belong to another language and another mode of thought. If you really wish to help a people use their language, and the ideas and modes of thought to which they are accustomed. You will thus help them to purify their conception of Truth as expressed in their own religion. THIS IS ONE OF THE AIMS OF THIS ORDER; TO BRING TO THE ATTENTION OF THE AMERICAN PEOPLE, AS SIMPLY AS POSSIBLE, THE PEARLS OF WISDOM IN THE TEACHINGS OF THE MASTER JESUS; PEARLS THAT HAVE BEEN OVERLAID WITH WORDY MISCONCEPTIONS SO LONG AS TO BE ALMOST UNRECOGNIZABLE.

There is a real necessity for the various presentations of Truth as given to the world; for just as the climate, flora and fauna of a country, and the language and customs of its people, vary in different parts of the world, so must Truth garb itself in habiliments suited to the modes of thought of the people to whom it is given. There is a deep occult reason underlying this law, and St. Paul recognized it when he said, "Be ye all things unto all men." There comes a time, however, in all organized bodies giving out spiritual teachings when some students will advance as far or farther than the leaders of the organization. And since it is only natural for such leaders to assume that they are more advanced than any of their students, inharmony and dissatisfaction or even secession result. In the development of all students a point is reached where they need the advanced, PERSONAL instruction not of any leaders—who are themselves but students—but of one who has at his command all knowledge and all wisdom, i.e., a Master of Wisdom.[1] It is in answer to this personal need that the Lodge of Masters has put forth THE ORDER OF THE 15 at this time. It comes as a direct response to the prayers of many, many hearts for more light, love, sympathy and personal guidance.

As this continent is to be the home of a new race which will ultimately perfect itself by the survival and interblending of the fittest of all races now existing, so must its religious thought be blended and purified so that it may emerge as a pure ray which has gathered unto itself the force from all its sub-rays.

THE ORDER OF THE 15 is put forth in an effort to awaken The Christ Love in the hearts of men, rather than to cater to the intellect or the desire for psychic powers; for only those who can correlate with The Christ power can be gathered together to form a nucleus in which this Power can manifest on earth. The aim of this Movement is especially to help all Christian people to find the deep, underlying, vital truths common to all religions in their own, and thus truly, and in the only way possible, prepare for an Universal Brotherhood on earth in which each Soul shall find the same vital

---

[1] It is understood, of course, that the Secretary does not answer the letters or compose the teachings. He is merely the Secretary in the ordinary sense of the word.

truths spoken in his own language, i.e., couched and taught in terms or the religion in which he was born.[1]

FINANCIAL OBLIGATIONS

Of course this Movement cannot be carried on without financial support, for the Law of Justice permits humanity to be helped only to the extent that, through its own efforts, it makes it possible for the help to reach it. If you feel an inner urge to study with us, and if you find that the lessons help you, you will naturally desire to help make it possible for other Souls to receive the same help. Therefore out of pure love and a desire to help others you will give as much as you can afford. Let all give according to their ability.[2]

---

[1] See Acts II, 6.
[2] See "Circular of Information" and "Special Notice."
Extra copies of this circular may be had by applying to the Secretary, Box 607, Denver, Colo., U.S.A.

www.ingramcontent.com/pod-product-compliance
Lightning Source LLC
Chambersburg PA
CBHW071503040426
42444CB00008B/1469